Kingdom, Church, and World:

Biblical Themes for Today

Howard A. Snyder

Wipf & Stock
PUBLISHERS
Eugene, Oregon

Wipf and Stock Publishers
199 West 8th Avenue, Suite 3
Eugene, Oregon 97401

Kingdom, Church, and World: Biblical Themes for Today
By Snyder, Howard A.
Copyright©1985 Snyder, Howard A.
ISBN: 1-57910-821-0
Publication date: November, 2001
Previously published by IVP, 1985.

Formerly titled 'A Kingdom Manifesto: Calling the Church to Live
Under God's Reign'

Other Books by Howard A. Snyder

The Problem of Wineskins: Church Structure in a Technological Age

The Community of the King

The Radical Wesley and Patterns for Church Renewal

Liberating the Church: The Ecology of Church and Kingdom

Signs of the Spirit: How God Reshapes the Church

The Divided Flame: Wesleyans and the Charismatic Movement
(with Daniel V. Runyon)

*Foresight: 10 Major Trends That Will Dramatically Affect
the Future of Christians and the Church (with Daniel V. Runyon)*

Models of the Kingdom

EarthCurrents: The Struggle for the World's Soul

Radical Renewal: The Problem of Wineskins Today
(Revised and expanded edition of The Problem of Wineskins)

Coherence in Christ: The Larger Meaning of Ecology

Global Good News: Mission in a New Context (editor)

Decoding the Church: The DNA of Christ's Body (with Daniel V. Runyon)

To
Mark
Jerilyn
Howard
Jonathan

May they see the kingdom—
present and future

Preface

Kingdom, Church, and World are all biblical themes. Yet Christians often wonder (and debate) how they relate to each other. Faithful churches and effective witness require that we know what the Kingdom of God is; that we be able to distinguish between the church and the kingdom; and that we grasp the kingdom role of the church in a troubled, sometimes terrorized world.

For various reasons, the gospel of the kingdom is not being heard in most North American churches today. Richard Halverson, former chaplain of the U.S. Senate, expressed the issue well: "I'm afraid evangelicalism is infected by the most subtle form of worldliness. It's the worldliness of Hollywood and Madison Avenue. . . . We operate as though the only thing worth doing in the world is what we can measure by numbers and dollars. We are not Kingdom of God people."[1] In 1984 George Barna identified a trend that is even clearer today: "[T]he integrity of the Christian faith is being severely tested by a social transformation of massive proportions. All available evidence indicates a body of believers unprepared to meet the challenge," being more *of* the world than different from it.[2]

Through its traditions the church too often voids the Word of God (Mk 7:13) and its kingdom message. Many people who have been converted to Jesus seem never to have been converted to the kingdom he proclaimed.

---

1. Interview with Richard C. Halverson, *Decision* 26:1 (January 1985), p. 24.

2. George Barna with William P. McKay, *Vital Signs: Emerging Social Trends and the Future of American Christianity* (Westchester, IL: Crossway Books, 1984), p. 5.

Yet there is hope! Signs of a recovery of the good news of God new order are sprouting everywhere. In fact, I believe there is more hop for a dramatic inbreaking of the Kingdom of God today than at any pre vious time in history. Much depends, however, on our hearing and obey ing the good news of the kingdom. I hope this book can help water th tender sprouts of new kingdom awareness.

The special mission of this book is dynamically to link church an kingdom without confusing the two – and to show what this means fc the world. Most writing on the church begins at some point other tha the kingdom and fails to show adequately what it means to be a kingdoı community. In my own Bible study, I began with the church but hav been pushed progressively to a kingdom theology precisely out of cor cern for a biblically faithful church.

This book arose initially out of an address I gave to leaders of th Evangelical Foreign Missions Association at their 1983 fall retreat. used the same material at our local church retreat that year, with surpri: ingly good results. The response encouraged me to expand the mant script into this somewhat fuller statement. The book was originall published as *A Kingdom Manifesto: Calling the Church to Live und* *God's Reign* (InterVarsity, 1985) and in England as *Kingdom Lifestyl* But *Kingdom, Church, and World* better captures the central thrust of th book for today.

This volume is in some ways a companion to my book, *The Commu nity of the King* (InterVarsity Press, 1977). That book dealt primaril with the church and secondarily with the kingdom; this one focuses pr marily on the kingdom and secondarily on the church. I deal at great length with the church in *Liberating the Church: The Ecology of Churc and Kingdom* (InterVarsity Press, 1983; Wipf & Stock, 1996), with th Kingdom of God in *Models of the Kingdom* (Abingdon, 1991; Wipf ‹ Stock, 2001), and with the world in *EarthCurrents: The Struggle for th World's Soul* (Abingdon, 1995).

Economic globalization, postmodernism, accelerating technolog genetic breakthroughs, war and terrorist attacks do not undercut the bas: thrust of this book. Rather, these developments make it more urgen This is a book, after all, about the Kingdom of God, not the Unite States. It is a book about the Church of Jesus Christ throughout th world, not the American Church. It is a book about the world, viewe not from the perspective of any one nation or ideology, but from the bil lical perspective of the Kingdom of God.

Introduction: A Key to All of Scripture

Jesus was always full of surprises, even with his disciples. Perhaps the biggest surprise was his news about the kingdom of God.

Jesus came announcing the kingdom, creating a stir. Through a brief span of public ministry he kept showing his disciples what the kingdom was really like. They understood only in part.

Later, risen from the dead, Jesus spent six weeks teaching his disciples more about the kingdom (Acts 1:3). He explained that his own suffering, death and resurrection were all part of the kingdom plan foretold by Old Testament prophets (Lk 24:44-47).

Now, after the resurrection, his disciples ask, "Are you *finally* going to set up your kingdom?" (paraphrasing Acts 1:6). How does Jesus respond? He says, in effect, "The time for the full flowering of the new order still remains a mystery to you; it's in God's hands. But . . . the Holy Spirit will give you the power to live the kingdom life *now*. So you are to be witnesses of the kingdom and its power from here to the very ends of the earth" (Acts 1:7-8).

And so it was, and so it has been. Today we are finally nearing the fulfillment of Jesus' prophecy that "this gospel of the kingdom will be preached in the whole world as a testimony to all nations" (Mt 24:14).

And so, as never before, it is time to speak of God's kingdom *now!*

This is no attempt to outguess God or pre-empt the sovereign mystery of the kingdom. The kingdom still and always remains in God's hands. So this book is not about "times or dates" (Acts

1:7)—a tempting but disastrous detour—but about the plain kingdom teachings which run throughout Scripture. My point is simply this: The Bible is full of teaching on the kingdom of God, and
the church has largely missed it. But in the providence of God
we may now have reached a time when the good news of the
kingdom can be heard and understood as never before. This is
due not to any one person, not to any human wisdom or insight,
but to God's own working in our day, bringing a new kingdom
consciousness.

Thus the theme of this book: The kingdom of God in Scripture
and its meaning for us today.

The kingdom of God is a key thread in Scripture, tying the
whole Bible together. It is not the only unifying theme, nor
should it replace other themes which are clearly biblical. Yet it
is a critically important theme, especially today. And its recent
resurgence in the church is, I believe, one of the most significant
developments of this century.[1]

Once you begin to look in Scripture for the theme of God's
reign or kingdom, it turns up everywhere! Take an example I
recently encountered in my own devotional study:
All you have made will praise you, O LORD;
    your saints will extol you.
They will tell of the glory of your kingdom
    and speak of your might,
so that all men may know of your mighty acts
    and the glorious splendor of your kingdom.
Your kingdom is an everlasting kingdom,
    and your dominion endures through all generations.
                                              (Ps 145:10-13)
This one psalm in fact contains a substantial theology of the
kingdom, stressing God's sovereign reign, his mighty acts, his
compassion and nearness to those who seek him, his righteousness and justice.

The kingdom is such a key theme of Scripture that Richard
Lovelace can say, "The Messianic Kingdom is not only the main

theme of Jesus' preaching; it is the central category unifying biblical revelation."[2] And John Bright comments, "The concept of the Kingdom of God involves, in a real sense, the total message of the Bible. . . . To grasp what is meant by the Kingdom of God is to come very close to the heart of the Bible's gospel of salvation."[3] As E. Stanley Jones wrote over four decades ago, Jesus' message "was the Kingdom of God. It was the center and circumference of all He taught and did. . . . The Kingdom of God is the master-conception, the master-plan, the master-purpose, the master-will that gathers everything up into itself and gives it redemption, coherence, purpose, goal."[4]

True, seeing the kingdom of God as the only unifying theme of Scripture could be misleading. Personally, I believe the overarching truth is the revelation of the nature and character of God (not merely his existence, which is clear from the created order—Rom 1:20). Here God's love, justice and holiness are central—the character of God's *person* in his triunity. Still the reign/rule of God is a key theme of Scripture, for the loving, just, holy God *rules* consistent with his character and in a way that produces the reflection of his character in all who willingly serve him.

So the kingdom is indeed a key strand running through the Bible. If it seems less evident in Paul's writings, that is because Paul often speaks of the kingdom in terms of the sovereign *plan* of God realized through Jesus Christ (as, for example, in Eph 1:10), and, for very good reasons, uses less kingdom language. But it is incorrect to say, as some have, that the kingdom theme "disappears" in Paul.[5]

This book is simply organized. In part one, we will explore seven biblical kingdom themes. In part two we will ask, "So what?" I show the pressing urgency of a theology of the kingdom both for the church and for public policy, suggesting what kingdom priorities might mean not only in the church but also in society at large. In the final chapter I suggest sixteen "Kingdom Operating Principles" which can help us build kingdom communities today.

Two final comments: First, I approach the kingdom theme as a pastor-theologian. The book is colored by my concern for the practical meaning of the kingdom in the daily life and witness of the church now. Second, I recognize certain inadequacies in the term *kingdom* for describing God's reign. Because of the currency of the term, I have decided to retain it, but I also use freely the words *reign of God, God's new order* and similar terms to counteract the mundaneness or misconceptions which *kingdom of God* may evoke for some.

First we ask: How is God's kingdom presented in Scripture? One way is as the realm of peace.

Part One
The Biblical Promise

1

The Peaceable Order

How beautiful on the mountains
are the feet of those who bring good news,
who proclaim peace,
who bring good tidings,
who proclaim salvation,
who say to Zion,
"Your God reigns!"

Isaiah 52:7

The Bible is full of God's kingdom. This is most clear, of course, in passages which speak directly of God's kingly rule. But kingdom surprises appear if we look at Scripture through a broader lens. We learn more about the kingdom when we view all of Scripture as the history of God's "economy" or plan to restore a fallen creation, bringing all God has made—woman, man and their total environment—to the fulfillment of his purposes under his sovereign reign.

Many Old Testament passages focus on God's kingdom, especially in the Psalms and the Prophets. Daniel, for example, sees in a vision the "son of man" appearing before the "Ancient of Days" where he is "given authority, glory and sovereign power; all peoples, nations and men of every language [worship] him. His dominion is an everlasting dominion that will not pass away, and his kingdom is one that will never be destroyed" (Dan 7:13-14). This vision clearly refers to Jesus Christ and lies behind several of the New Testament passages which speak of Christ's work, including some which do not use the word *kingdom*.

The significance of such passages is sharpened when we note several related Old Testament themes. I find that seven themes, in particular, shed light on God's kingdom. These are *peace, land, house, city, justice, Sabbath* and *Jubilee*. We will explore each of these briefly. In each case we will look first at the Old Testament background and then the New Testament development of the theme.

Various church traditions have stressed one or another biblical theme, using it as a key in interpreting Scripture. The following themes, for instance, have all been used in this way: covenant, the people of God, law, holiness, the Holy Spirit, the Messiah. Each of these is an important strand in Scripture, and one's particular theology will vary in focus and accent depending on which is stressed. Each of these themes should, in fact, be incorporated into a biblical theology, and each helps us understand the kingdom of God. Conversely, using the kingdom as an integrating framework sheds light on the meaning of these themes for the life of God's people in the world. But I find the seven themes treated here of special help in understanding the meaning of God's kingdom for today.

Of all the streams of biblical truth none is more appealing than *shalom*, peace!

The Kingdom as Shalom

Shalom, usually translated "peace," is one of the great words of the Old Testament. It occurs some 350 times[1] and clearly underlies the concept of peace found in the New Testament, as we shall see.

Shalom is so woven into the fabric of the Old Testament that to touch virtually any strand of Bible history or theology is to meet it. As Douglas Harris notes, "The root meaning is 'to be whole, sound, safe.' The fundamental idea is totality. God is the source and ground for *shalom.* Anything that contributes to this wholeness makes for *shalom.* Anything that stands in the way disrupts *shalom.*"[2] In Bishop John Taylor's words, the biblical vision of *shalom* "meant a dancing kind of inter-relationship, seeking something more free than equality, more generous than equity, the ever-shifting equipoise of a life-system."[3]

The Old Testament teaches that God's plan is to bring a universal peace *(shalom)* to his creation. This means more than the absence of conflict and immensely more than "inner peace" or "peace of mind." In the Old Testament sense, *shalom* might be called an ecological concept. It carries the sense of harmony, right relationship and the proper functioning of all elements in the environment.[4] "At root it means 'well-being,' with a strong emphasis on the material side," and it is closely connected in the Old Testament with covenant.[5] The Garden of Eden before the Fall provides a good model. This *shalom* is "every man sitting under his own vine and under his own fig tree," with none to make them afraid. (Compare 1 Kings 4:25 and Micah 4:4—an image of the eschatological fulfillment of the peace enjoyed under King Solomon.)

Shalom is, of course, directly tied to the kingly rule of the Messiah in passages such as Isaiah 9:6-7. The Messiah is the "Prince of Peace," and "of the increase of his government and peace there will be no end." The clear link in the Old Testament of *shalom* with God's reign suggests that the dozens of references to the word and ideal should be studied thoroughly for their kingdom content.

I have called *shalom* an ecological reality. In the Old Testament *peace* is decidedly a this-worldly concept, grounded in the very physical nature of God's creation. It is harmony and wholeness. In bringing peace, God brings healing: "I will bring health and healing to [the city]; I will heal my people and will let them enjoy abundant peace and security" (Jer 33:6).

The New Testament builds on the *shalom* promises of the Old

Testament when it speaks of the gospel of peace. The apostle
Paul, for instance, tells us that the kingdom of God is "righteousness, peace and joy in the Holy Spirit" (Rom 14:17). Peace is at
the heart of God's reign.

The New Testament theme of peace ties the kingdom directly
to Jesus Christ. To know Jesus is to be in the kingdom. At Jesus'
birth the angels announced "peace on earth" as the meaning of
Jesus' coming (Lk 2:14). Jesus is the Prince of Peace (Is 9:6); like
Melchizedek he is "King of Peace" (Heb 7:2). God reigns through
Jesus Christ, and the meaning of that reign is peace.

In the New Testament we see first, and most basically, that
peace comes through the life and work of Jesus Christ. He is our
peace. Through him we are reconciled to God, receiving the
forgiveness of our sins, and so we have peace. The richest passage here is Ephesians 2:14-17: "For he himself is our peace, who
has made the two one and has destroyed the barrier, the dividing
wall of hostility. . . . His purpose was to create in himself one new
man out of the two, thus making peace, and in this one body to
reconcile both of them to God through the cross, by which he
put to death their hostility. He came and preached peace to you
who were far away and peace to those who were near. For
through him we both have access to the Father by one Spirit."

Jesus is our peace, our *shalom*! When we remember the full Old
Testament richness of peace, we begin to feel what this means.
All the promises of *shalom* are being answered in Jesus Christ.

But how and in what sense? Ephesians 2:14-17 is closely related
to Ephesians 1:10, Colossians 1:20 and 2 Corinthians 5:19, all of
which speak of the reconciling, uniting work of God through
Jesus Christ. In these passages we see that to unite all things in
Christ, to bring peace, and to reconcile are all different ways of
saying the same thing. *Reconciliation means making peace.* United
under the headship of Jesus, everything in heaven and earth
becomes reconciled, coming to peace with God and with itself.
"For God was pleased to have all his fullness dwell in him, and
through him to reconcile to himself all things, whether things on

earth or things in heaven, by making peace through his blood, shed on the cross" (Col 1:19-20).

The peace which Jesus brings is rooted in the Old Testament promises. It therefore clearly means universal *shalom* throughout the whole created order—not just absence of conflict but harmony, balance and health. It involves, in Paul's words, "all things." Peace in the New Testament is "the state of final fulfillment, the normal state of the new creation." "The 'healthy' or normal state which corresponds to the will of God is not to be limited to the soul or even to man. It extends basically to the universe as a whole."[6] Peace is, first of all, peace with God, reaching out from personal experience to the whole creation. God is "reconciling the world [the cosmos] to himself in Christ" (2 Cor 5:19).

We miss the full kingdom significance of peace unless we see it in this broadest scope. There are other aspects, as we will see, but at heart peace is the full cosmic reconciliation which has always been the final goal and end of God's promises.

In Jesus Christ, peace becomes not only visible; it becomes specific. Watching Jesus, we see what peace really means: Martha and Mary, John and the disciples, blind Bartimaeus, Zacchaeus, Jairus. Clearly, peace is relational: it is always a pattern of peace *with*, or peace *between*, or peace *among*, as these examples show. And since the Bible sees the world ecologically, with all aspects of creation linked to all others, peace in the kingdom sense necessarily reaches to the "harmonizing" of every reality and relationship under God's authority.

The peace passages in the New Testament underscore this concreteness. In Ephesians 2, Paul says Jesus has destroyed the "dividing wall of hostility" between Jew and Gentile. Peace here is specific: Jesus creates a new, reconciled community where Jews and Gentiles meet as sisters and brothers in one new peaceable family. Throughout his writings, Paul carefully notes that it is not just the Jew/Gentile hostility, but *all* hostility which has been overcome by Jesus. So now "there is neither Jew nor Greek, slave nor free, male nor female, for you are all one in Christ Jesus" (Gal 3:28). This is the great, practical application of peace in the New Testament, the key link between kingdom and church. The kingdom breaks in now through a community of believers where peace is the trademark. *In God's kingdom plan, peace is both the final goal of the kingdom and the present experience of the community of Jesus' disciples.*

Jesus is the key. He has brought peace between God and humankind. He reconciles through life, death and resurrection. "Therefore, since we have been justified through faith, we have peace with God through our Lord Jesus Christ" (Rom 5:1). Through repentance and faith, men and women are born again into a restored fellowship with God and with sisters and brothers in Christ. Having been reconciled, they are called to work out and live a life of peace. They are to be a reconciled and reconciling fellowship.

The New Testament stresses our calling to build the peaceful community. Paul says we should "make every effort to do what leads to peace and to mutual edification" (Rom 14:19). We must "live at peace with everyone" (Rom 12:18), striving "to live in peace with all men and to be holy" (Heb 12:14). Christians, notes James, should be "peacemakers who sow in peace" and "raise a harvest of righteousness" or justice (Jas 3:18). These words simply reinforce Jesus' own: "Blessed are the peacemakers, for they will be called [children] of God" (Mt 5:9). Christians are kingdom people when, having found peace with God through Jesus, they build a peaceful community and become agents of God's *shalom* in the world.

Jesus says to his disciples at the Last Supper, "Peace I leave with you; my peace I give you. I do not give to you as the world gives" (Jn 14:27). And again: "I have told you these things, so that in me you may have peace. In this world you will have trouble. But take heart! I have overcome the world" (Jn 16:33). Then, following the resurrection, Jesus tells his disciples, "Peace be with you! As the Father has sent me, I am sending you" (Jn 20:21).

These are tremendous words of comfort and assurance. They take on even deeper significance when we remember the Old Testament promises of a kingdom of *shalom*. Jesus, the only one who fully knows the Father, gives us his peace, and sends us out with his peace—a peace from God, not of mere human making. Because we have been given peace with God through Jesus Christ, we can be his peacemakers in the world. We are to announce the peace of forgiveness and regeneration, and also the peace throughout all creation which flows from the reconciling work of Jesus. Peace with God, through Jesus Christ: Here is the basis of both evangelism and social ministry, both justification and justice. For this is all the work of Christ the King. Jesus gives us peace "not of this world," but a peace which overcomes and comes over the world.

In sum, peace in the New Testament has the same meaning as in the Old, but now finds its focus and means in the person of Jesus Christ and the New Covenant in his blood. Peace loses none of its cosmic or this-worldly force in the New Testament. But now its basis and practical meaning for daily life are clarified. We now see how the great promises for peace on earth will come about: through Jesus Christ, and through the Christian community, his body on earth.

But we must guard against any either/or thinking: Peace on earth *or* peace with God; inner peace *or* outward peace. God's peace is one, and his kingdom plan is one. In no sense does the New Testament pull in the boundaries of peace, reducing it to personal experience only. No, the circle remains just as stunningly vast and concrete as ever. But now the center is defined. It is "peace with God through our Lord Jesus Christ"— first of all in human experience, but extending to the "reconciliation of all things," which always remains the goal of the kingdom (Rom 5:1; Col 1:20).

"Peace, in the scriptural sense," said Wesley, "implies all blessings, temporal and eternal."[7] According to Walter Brueggemann, "*Shalom* is the substance of the biblical vision of one community embracing all creation. It refers to all those resources and factors which make communal harmony joyous and effective"; it is "well-being of a material, physical, historical kind."[8] In this sense, says Brueggemann, Jesus' "acts of healing the sick, forgiving the guilty, raising the dead, and feeding the hungry are all actions of re-establishing God's will for *shalom* in a world gone chaotic by callous self-seeking."[9] They are signs of the kingdom and revelations of the character of God's new order.

Jesus warns us, however, that peace may not come peaceably. Precisely because he is the Prince of Peace in a violent world, his coming means not peace but division (Lk 12:51). War is still raging, and our efforts at peace will enrage the enemies of peace. Our task is to have peace among ourselves and work for peace, trusting in the promise that "the God of peace will soon crush Satan under your feet" (Rom 16:20).

The Narrow Gate

One evening my seven-year-old son and I walked through a little patch of woods and came out on an open field. The sun was westering; the sky was serenely laced with blue and gold. Birds flitted in the trees. We talked about peace, the future and the kingdom of God. Somehow we both sensed, despite our differences in age and understanding, that God desires peace and that what he desires he will bring. Someday, we said and knew, all the world will be like this magic moment. But not without cost and struggle.

Jesus urges: "Enter through the narrow gate." For "small is the gate and narrow the road that leads to life, and only a few find it" (Mt 7:13-14). The kingdom of God is life in abundance (Jn 10:10), but the way to that life is through the narrow gate of faith and obedience to Jesus Christ. If Christians today want to experience the peaceable order of the kingdom, they must learn and live God's way to peace.

We will explore the broader issues of peace more fully in part two of this book, but I would suggest here a couple of things which *shalom* means practically for the church today.

1. *The church must be at peace with itself.* If peace is not the mark of the church's own life, it will not be the mark of its ministry in the world.

A peaceable community is one where people are being reconciled with one another. Petty resentments, gossip, unkind comments and lingering jealousies have no place in a community of faith. The church cannot create a peace in the world which it does not experience in itself. Broader witness will suffer if these internal dimensions of peace are not faced.

2. *We must present a gospel of peace to the world,* not a message of violence, distrust, discord and alienation. The church must show that only in Jesus can people and nations find real peace. This says something about the link between the church's evangelism and broader social witness. Jesus is the Prince of Peace who brings reconciliation *now* in all areas of alienation (social, racial, political, personal), as well as peace with God. The church can show this by combining in one community both personal evangelism and involvement in peace concerns locally and internationally.

These are some of the present dimensions of peace which point toward the fuller, final *shalom* of the kingdom.

God loves *shalom.* Already he is subtly, secretly, surely bringing his new peaceable order. So he calls us to be peacemakers now, in the conviction that in time he will decisively bring the fullness of *shalom* to his creation.

The kingdom of God is peace!

2

The Promised Land

May the nations be glad and sing for joy,
for you rule the peoples justly
and guide the nations of the earth.
May the peoples praise you, O God;
may all the peoples praise you.
Then the land will yield its harvest,
and God, our God, will bless us.
God will bless us,
and all the ends of the earth will fear him.
Psalm 67:4-7

Wendell Berry is a remarkable man. Poet, philosopher, Kentucky farmer, Berry has been a prophet of the land. His life is so tied to the rhythms of nature that to read him is to feel transported out of the Technological Society.

Berry sees two contrasting attitudes toward the land: the nurturer and the exploiter. He writes,

I conceive a strip-miner to be a model exploiter, and as a model nurturer I take the old-fashioned idea or ideal of a farmer. The exploiter is a specialist, an expert; the nurturer is not. The standard of the exploiter is efficiency; the standard of the nurturer is care. The exploiter's goal is money, profit; the nurturer's goal is health—his land's health, his own, his family's, his community's, his country's. . . . The exploiter wishes to earn as much as possible by as little work as possible; the nurturer expects, certainly, to have a decent living from his work, but his characteristic wish is to work *as well* as possible. The competence of the exploiter is in organization; that of the nurturer is in order—a human order, that is, that accommodates itself both to other order and to mystery. The exploiter typically serves an institution or organization; the nurturer serves land, household, community, place. The exploiter thinks in terms of numbers, quantities, "hard facts"; the nurturer in terms of character, condition, quality, kind.[1]

Thinking Christians will quickly see that the nurturing attitude is more nearly the biblical one. Yet often it is not the way we live. And this is part of the reason the church today has trouble really understanding the kingdom. A whole new dimension to God's new order emerges as we look at what Scripture says about land.

In the Old Testament, land is closely tied to *shalom*. God promises his people a land where they will dwell in peace: "I will grant peace in the land, and you will lie down and no one will make you afraid" (Lev 26:6).

When God begins to form a people, he promises them land. God sends Abram to "the land I will show you" and says that through him "all peoples on earth will be blessed" (Gen 12:1-3). Making his covenant with Abraham, God promises "the whole land of Canaan" as "an everlasting possession" (Gen 17:8). "I will make you a community of peoples," God promises Jacob, "and I will give this land as an everlasting possession" (Gen 48:4). Repeatedly God speaks of the land: "I will remember the land," he says (Lev 26:42).

Walter Brueggemann has shown the key place of land for biblical faith in his book *The Land*. The Bible is not, Brueggemann argues, the story of God and his people only, but of God, his people and the land. Land, both as "actual earthly turf" and as symbol of rootedness or "historical belonging," Brueggemann believes, is "a central, if not *the central theme* of biblical faith."[2] Keeping the biblical focus on land before us "will protect us from excessive spiritualization, so that we recognize that the yearning for land is always a serious historical enterprise concerned with historical power and belonging."[3]

The central place of land in God's economy is striking ecologically. In both Scripture and ecology, the ideal is man and woman living at home on the land in an environment of balance, harmony and mutual dependence. It is neither biblically nor ecologically sound to view humankind as living independently from the land. And it is fundamentally unecological, both spiritually and physically, to attempt autonomous life divorced or alienated from the land.

The close link between land and God's messianic promises helps us understand God's kingdom now. God cares for the environment in which we live and on which we depend. He intends to redeem women and men *with* their environment, not *out of* it. God loves all his creation, not just the human part of it. Psalm 65:9 says God cares for the land; he waters it and enriches it abundantly. This is fully consistent, incidentally, with the Incarnation.

What is the Promised Land for Christians? We may think that the Old Testament sense of land is left behind as we move into the New Testament, or that the gospel says little about land in the Old Testament sense. But let's take a closer look.

We noted earlier that the Old Testament is the story of God's people *and* God's land. God promises his people a secure, peaceful, physical environment where they can live forever. The land will be their inheritance.[4] The place to begin, then, in the New Testament is with passages which recall God's earlier promises about land. Some key passages are Acts 3:25, 7:3 and 13:19; Romans 9:17; Ephesians 6:3; and Hebrews 11:7.

Four of these passages quote directly from the Old Testament. Preaching in Acts 3, Peter cites Genesis 22:18 and 26:4 when he says, "Through your offspring all peoples on earth will be blessed" (Acts 3:25). This is, of course, God's promise to Abraham, now fulfilled in those who accept Jesus as the Messiah.

Later, in Acts 7, Stephen quotes God's words to Abraham in Genesis 12:1: "Leave your country [or land, *gē*] and your people . . . and go to the land I will show you" (Acts 7:3).

Similarly, Paul quotes Exodus 9:16 in Romans 9:17 ("that my name might be proclaimed in all the earth") and in Ephesians 6:3 reminds children that they must obey their parents "that it may go well with you and that you may enjoy long life on the earth" (quoting Deut 5:16).

Several passages refer specifically to the Promised Land. Paul notes that the land was given to God's people as their inheritance (Acts 13:19), and Hebrews 11:9 says that Abraham "made his home in the promised land." Later the same chapter notes that all the Old Testament heroes of faith "admitted that they were aliens and strangers on earth" (Heb 11:13).

These passages reveal a significant clue as to the meaning of God's kingdom now. Although some use the word *land* and others *earth*, the Greek New Testament uses the same word: *gē* (from which we get the prefix, "geo-"). Thus in the New Testament *earth* and *land* are the same.

Could it be, then, that the Promised Land of the Old Testament becomes the whole earth in the kingdom of God? Let us see.

The word *land* or *earth* (*gē*) occurs 248 times in the New Testament, especially in the Gospels, Acts and the Revelation.[5] It means first of all earth or soil; a sower plants seeds in the earth. By extension, the word means land or the whole earth. Thus it has essentially the same range of meanings that in English *land* and *earth*, ·combined, have. The key point is that the word designates both actual physical soil and the entire planet. The heavens and the earth are seen as God's creation and so share in God's redeeming work: "Redemption extends to the furthest corner of the physical realm."[6]

Already in the Old Testament the promise of land as an inheritance was tied to the larger promise of blessing for all the earth. God tells Jacob, "I will give you and your descendants the land on which you are lying. . . . All peoples on earth will be blessed through you and your offspring" (Gen 28:13-14; see Is 60:21). God promises land—actual, physical turf—and then says that through his people the whole earth, all land and peoples, will be blessed.

The New Testament builds on this foundation. Land does not at all disappear in the New Testament. Nor is it vaporized into a spiritual heaven. Rather it becomes the whole earth, understood not merely symbolically or cosmically (and certainly not spiritually), but as the actual physical environment given men and women as their home.

From this perspective, several New Testament passages take on new kingdom significance. Jesus says in Matthew 5:5, for instance, "Blessed are the meek, for they will inherit the earth" (a quotation from Ps 37:11).[7]

The context here is the Sermon on the Mount, where Jesus clearly is speaking about the kingdom of God. The meek, the poor in spirit, the merciful: these are the children of the kingdom. And it is they, the children of the kingdom, who will "inherit the earth." To "inherit the land" is to receive the fulfillment of God's promises that his people would be blessed, would receive a "land flowing with milk and honey," and would be a blessing to the whole earth. God's people, then, the children of the kingdom, will in the end receive the promised inheritance, not just the Promised Land of Israel, but the whole earth. God's people will extend throughout the world. They will be given the whole earth as their peaceful environment. And, in fact, they have now received the whole earth as part of their stewardship.

In Acts 1:8, Jesus tells his disciples that they will be his witnesses "in Jerusalem, and in all Judea and Samaria, and to the ends of the earth." This is, in part, how Matthew 5:5 will be fulfilled. The land is still God's land, though now alienated and polluted physically and morally. But God's people will be witnesses throughout the earth. In the power of the Holy Spirit they will show forth the reality of Jesus Christ, spreading the good

news and winning people to faith in Jesus; forming communities of believers who live the Jesus life, who model the kingdom. So the kingdom will begin to spread throughout the earth
in preparation for its final manifestation with the return of
Jesus Christ. Through faith in Jesus and through life together
in Jesus-style communities, the children of the kingdom—the
meek, the poor, the peacemakers, the justice seekers—will extend the kingdom witness to the ends of the earth. This is the
beginning of the reclaiming of the land for the kingdom of
God.

We are guarded against an easy optimism, however, by Peter's words that "the present heavens and earth are reserved for
fire, being kept for the day of judgment and destruction of
ungodly men" (2 Pet 3:7). At that time "the elements will be
destroyed by fire, and the earth and everything in it will be laid
bare" (2 Pet 3:10). "But in keeping with his promise we are
looking forward to a new heaven and a new earth *[gē]*, the
home of righteousness" (2 Pet 3:13).[8]

Here we face the certainty and mystery of judgment. The
earth will undergo a change, a refining by fire—but it will not
be annihilated! The whole creation will finally be set free (Rom
8:21). As with our bodies, so with the earth: "The perishable
must clothe itself with the imperishable" (1 Cor 15:53). We
know that "flesh and blood cannot inherit the kingdom of
God" (1 Cor 15:50), but the whole created order will undergo
a fundamental change, a transformation, a redemption. And
the model for all this is the historical death and resurrection
of Jesus Christ. The resurrected body of Jesus is the model, the
proof, the demonstrated power and the hope of God's final
redemption of this earth—an earth just as physical as the mole-
cules that made up Jesus' body.

The book of Revelation graphically climaxes this theme of
the new heaven and earth. God's people have been made "a
kingdom and priests to serve our God, and they will reign on
the earth *[gē]*" (Rev 5:10). We will see "a new heaven and a new

earth" (Rev 21:1) which will be the final, complete, glorious fulfillment of all the biblical promises about land.

What does this mean for God's kingdom now? It means we are tenants on God's land, for which God is concerned and for which he has a plan that involves our stewardship of the land. We never own real estate: God is the owner. Yet we are assured that already in Jesus Christ all things are ours, whether present or future (1 Cor 3:22).

The New Testament says "love not the world," but nowhere are we told not to love the earth! We should love the land as God does. We are to care for it, for it is the environment of the kingdom. It is the soil of *shalom*, the place where God is working. And it will be redeemed, transformed, turned into a land of stable peace, a land flowing with milk and honey.

What, then, is the Promised Land for Christians? Traditionally we have viewed it as heaven in a very spiritual, nonmaterial sense. But is it not, rather, the new earth God is bringing? The Promised Land is not earth left behind, but heaven come down. Not mansions in the sky by and by but a home on earth. The heavenly city descends to earth (Rev 21:2).

In one sense, we already live in the Promised Land. God has given us this earth to care for. Kingdom people must tend the earth—first, because God created it; second, because it is our environment, the present location of kingdom activity; and, finally, because this earth will be transformed into the new earth—the very locale of the kingdom!

This is the present meaning of land for the kingdom of God. While the kingdom is primarily God's reign, still there is a locale of that reign, a land of the kingdom—the place of God's dominion. And it is the whole earth.

The Narrow Gate

If the Promised Land is the whole earth, what does this mean for the church today? Here are some examples.

1. *We must present a gospel and a Savior that are concerned with*

earth as well as heaven. Jesus must be presented as the Messiah who "will not falter or be discouraged till he establishes justice on earth" (Is 42:4) as well as the one who "was pierced for our transgressions" and "crushed for our iniquities" (Is 53:5). This is even better news than the good news Christians often preach!

2. *We must learn to love, respect and care for the environment,* not merely exploit it. Christians should have profound reverence for the intricate world God has given us, not destroying it but conserving it. North American Christians, especially, must become much more knowledgeable about environmental concerns. We should know at least as much about how to save the earth as about how to save money.

3. Relatedly, *we should practice environmental sensitivity in our daily lives.* This means frugality and simplicity in both family and church life. Church buildings, if needed, should reflect care for the natural world around us, simple beauty and energy efficiency. Why shouldn't Christians be in the vanguard of environmental awareness, even in the buildings they use?

4. *We should work for the just use of land.* Land is a stewardship given to all humanity in trust. It is not a commodity to be hoarded or monopolized for the wealth of the few, which biblically is gross injustice. Christians should work for proper stewardship of all land for the benefit of the whole human family.

Thinking of land reminds me of my boyhood in southern Michigan—walking the furrows of fresh-turned earth, watching ants scurry to repair a disturbed anthill, pondering the tiny creatures in the swamp "out back." The earth is good! More, it is marvelous, and wondrously intricate. It is more than a parable of a heavenly reality, and vastly more than a poor reflection of some Platonic ideal world. The earth is the real, good, exciting work of God, given us to enjoy and care for. And in God's economy, the children of the kingdom will inherit the earth (Mt 5:5).

About the age of fourteen, I found one day the nest of a rose-breasted grosbeak just a couple of feet off the path of a familiar trail through the woods. What a sight to see! The mother flew from the nest, rustling leaves and revealing the center of her little world, speckled eggs in a circlet of twigs. All summer I watched the brilliant male and his mate, fully at home in that patch of woods, yet so vulnerable to the human community around them.

God still loves gardens, trees, birds. St. Francis was right about that. And God's commission to Adam and Eve in Eden "to work it and take care of it" (Gen 2:15) is not just ancient history or poetry. It is a revelation of the character of the kingdom and of the King. God still has an inheritance for his people; there is still a Promised Land.

3

The House of God

The LORD declares to you that the LORD himself
will establish a house for you: When
your days are over and you rest with your
fathers, I will raise up your offspring to succeed
you, who will come from your own body,
and I will establish his kingdom.

2 Samuel 7:11-12

God wants to *dwell* with his people—to make his home among them. This is the central meaning of the tabernacle and the temple in the Old Testament.

Consider the exciting implications of Exodus 25:8-9: "Have them make a sanctuary for me, and I will dwell among them. Make this tabernacle and all its furnishings exactly like the pattern I will show you." Compare this with the picture of the culminated kingdom in Revelation 21:3-4: "And I heard a loud voice from the throne saying, 'Now the dwelling of God is with men, and he will live with them. They will be his people, and God himself will be with them and be their God. He will wipe every tear from their eyes. There will be no more death or mourning

or crying or pain, for the old order of things has passed away.' "
God's plan, and the intent of his dwelling with his chosen people,
is that he should reign *over* and *with* them in an environment of
peace, justice and love.

I have traced the theme of God's tabernacle and temple, and
more broadly of the "house" of God, throughout the Bible. It has
been a fascinating study. Part of the fruit of that study is summa-
rized in the chapter "Churches, Temples and Tabernacles" in
The Problem of Wineskins.[1] Some of my essential conclusions are
these: While both the tabernacle and the temple represent God's
dwelling among his people, the tabernacle is an especially
powerful symbol of God's presence among his pilgrim people on
earth. For the present, God's people are sojourners in the land,
and thus they are uniquely placed to understand and identify
with the poor, the displaced, the refugees. God journeys with his
pilgrim people—his earthly presence represented by the
tabernacle, but his transcendent power shown by the pillar of fire
and smoke accompanying it.

In contrast to the tabernacle, the temple points ahead to the
fulfillment of God's purposes in the new order of the kingdom.
Nowhere is this clearer than in 2 Samuel 7 and the prophecy of
Haggai. Solomon's temple and kingdom become the symbol for
the final kingdom when Jesus Christ, the son of David who per-
fectly fulfills the promises of 2 Samuel 7:11-16 and Haggai 2:6-
9, will reign. In the words of Nathan the prophet, the son of
David "will build a house for my Name, and I will establish the
throne of his kingdom forever" (2 Sam 7:13). Temple and king,
house and kingdom—they go together in God's plan.[2] Thus
house, temple and tabernacle have kingdom significance.

The themes of house, temple and tabernacle are fulfilled dramatically in the New Testament. The Word is made flesh and
"tabernacles" among us (Jn 1:14). When Jesus speaks of rebuilding the temple in three days, "the temple he had spoken of was
his body" (Jn 2:21). More than that, through his life, death, resurrection and continuing reign, Jesus forms a new family, the

church, to be his living house and temple on earth (2 Cor 6:16; Heb 3:6; 1 Pet 2:5; among many other passages). This is most graphically depicted in Ephesians 2:19-22: "Consequently, you are no longer foreigners and aliens, but fellow citizens with God's people and members of God's household, built on the foundation of the apostles and prophets, with Christ Jesus himself as the chief cornerstone. In him the whole building is joined together and rises to become a holy temple in the Lord. And in him you too are being built together to become a *dwelling* in which God lives by his Spirit."

The Holy Spirit is speaking here of a new house, a new kind of family. The wall between Jew and Gentile has crumbled; Jesus brings a new peace powerful enough to unite in one house folks who, by the world's values, hate one another. This is the church, God's special household, created as sign and agent of *shalom* in our whole earth home.

To examine this truth fully requires studying the biblical word for "house, family, household" *(oikos)* in some depth. Since I have already done this elsewhere, it will be sufficient here to give a brief summary.[3]

In the Bible, the idea of "house of God" is used in two senses: the whole created order as God's house or dwelling, and God's chosen people in a special sense, called and empowered to a stewardship or economy *(oikonomia)* of caring for the earth and serving as agents of reconciliation to bring all creation back to God. Thus God's plan *(oikonomia)* for the fullness of time is "to unite [reconcile] all things in [Jesus Christ], things in heaven and things on earth" (Eph 1:10 RSV).

The church, then, is the house of God, and the whole created order is also God's house. The unique role of the church, as Jesus' body on earth, is to be the visible household where God's peace now reigns and the point of the inbreaking and accomplishing of God's reign throughout God's house in the broadest sense—the whole cosmos. Clearly, the kingdom as God's house in this sense is fully consistent with the New Testament meaning of the other themes we have been noting. God's house or family is to be the agent of *shalom* in God's land, the earth, to enact justice for the oppressed, to announce God's reign, to work for the full coming of the city of God with its final Sabbath rest.

The Narrow Gate

This truth has tremendous practical impact for the daily life of God's people in the world, as I have attempted to show in *Liberating the Church* and will show further in the remaining chapters of this book. God is building his house; he is bringing his kingdom. The church is called to live as a microcosm of the kingdom, a model house for full reconciliation throughout God's creation.

Here are some specific, practical implications of the house theme:

1. *The church should rediscover the home as the center of her life as the community of God's people.* The home is the place where the routine activities of life are carried out, and this is where life together as God's family should be experienced. The biblical pattern seems to be "the church in your house."

The most basic meetings of the Christian community should be in homes. Large-group worship and some training functions may require larger space, but the home is the primary place where the reality of the church is experienced. Homes often provide ideal settings for fellowship, study, prayer, small-group worship and evangelism. Also, many believers find that living together in shared households provides an enjoyable and more economical way to live and is a significant aid to ministry. Not all Christians are called to this, but it is a good option for many.

2. *The church should cultivate the sense of being the family* (oikos) *of God.* In these days of single-parent families, single-person households and the disintegration of family life, the church needs to see and experience itself as an extended family where every believer really is "at home." It must grow also in its sense of being one family around the world—a family where the sufferings of some are the sufferings of all and where resources are

shared freely across racial and national boundaries.

3. *The church must affirm God's love for the whole human family and the whole created order.* God is Father not only of those who believe; he is the Father "from whom his whole family in heaven and on earth derives its name" (Eph 3:15). True Christians are those who, in the words of John Wesley, exhibit a "disinterested love for all mankind." Christians are called to demonstrate God's justice, mercy and truth toward all people everywhere—not just to our own kind. Every church should therefore be involved in both world evangelism and world justice. All deserve to hear, and all deserve to eat.

I admit I love to look at houses. The other day Jan and I walked up through the park, along the Chicago River. We returned through an area of beautiful homes. Healthy trees, neat yards, and solid houses of brick and stone blended into a scene of charm and elegance; human creativity in God's world. "I like nice houses," said my wife. "I guess I'm just a materialist."

Lopsided luxury is a sin against God's justice, but beauty and creativity are not. God is the great materialist, but he is more. He is the great architect—the builder of a house and kingdom—and human inventiveness often shadows the Divine Creator.

What a privilege to be part of God's house! What joy to know that sharing here and now in the family of God is concrete work toward the final house which is nothing less than the kingdom of God.

4

The City of the King

Great is the LORD, and most worthy of praise,
in the city of our God, his holy mountain.
It is beautiful in its loftiness,
the joy of the whole earth.
Like the utmost heights of Zaphon is Mount Zion,
the city of the Great King.
God is in her citadels;
he has shown himself to be her fortress.
                                    Psalm 48:1-3

God wills his peaceful reign in the city. The kingdom of God brings the city of God.

The Bible, some say, begins in a garden and ends in a city. More accurately, the Bible begins with a garden as the setting for ideal human community with God and ends with a city which is also a garden, as we shall see. This imagery points to the final culmination of the kingdom of God.

The Bible is a book about cities, not just about sheep and vineyards. An urban theme runs through Scripture, as pointed out in recent years by a number of people and explored by Jacques Ellul in *The Meaning of the City*.[1] This theme is significant in its own right, especially in this age of urbanization, but it also clearly links with God's rule or reign. The Bible is clear that God's new order directly concerns what happens in cities, in A.D. 2000 as well as in 2000 B.C.

The city theme recurs in the Bible in several forms, both positively and negatively (for instance, Babel/Babylon versus Zion/Jerusalem). This urban perspective comes to focus especially in the theme of Zion, the city of David, the city of the king, from which all nations will be ruled justly and to which all nations will come.

The first reference to a city in the Bible is Genesis 4:17. After killing his brother, Cain builds a city and names it after his son Enoch. In Ellul's view, the city is Cain's "substitute Eden," and throughout history represents humanity's attempt to build security apart from God. "For God's Eden [Cain] substitutes his own; for the goal given to his life by God, he substitutes a goal chosen by himself—just as he substituted his own security for God's. Such is the act by which Cain takes his destiny on his own shoulders, refusing the hand of God in his life."[2] This line of development leads directly to Babel and Babylon, the height of human rebellion, technology and attempted autonomy.

But a contrasting urban theme emerges in the Old Testament: the city of God. This is, first of all, the city of David, the city of God's chosen king from whose line will come the Son of David. Anointed king over all Israel, David conquers the Jebusite city Jerusalem. "David captured the fortress of Zion, the City of David. . . . David then took up residence in the fortress and called it the City of David. . . . And he became more and more powerful, because the LORD God Almighty was with him" (2 Sam 5:7-10; 1 Chron 11:5-9).

As the Davidic kingdom comes to symbolize the future kingdom of God, so the city of David becomes the city of God. The theme is developed poetically:

There is a river whose streams make glad the city of God,
  the holy place where the Most High dwells. (Ps 46:4)
Great is the LORD, and most worthy of praise,
  in the city of our God, his holy mountain. (Ps 48:1)

Glorious things are said of you,
   O city of God:
"I will record Rahab and Babylon
   among those who acknowledge me—
Philistia too, and Tyre, along with Cush—
   and will say, 'This one was born in Zion.' " (Ps 87:3-4)

Historically Jerusalem was destroyed by Babylon because the people broke the covenant. But God did not forget his covenant, and the vision of God's city, the holy city, remained as an anchor for the people's hope in a merciful and sovereign Lord. And in exile, awaiting God's deliverance, the people are told, "Seek the peace and prosperity of the city to which I have carried you into exile. Pray to the LORD for it, because if it prospers, you too will prosper" (Jer 29:7). Here is a snapshot of God's people on earth, living in the alien (or alienated) city, but serving the God who promises finally a city of peace and tells them to seek the *shalom* of the city where God has placed them for the present. Daniel, in fact, receives God's promise that the holy city will be rebuilt and the Anointed One will come while he is living as an exile in Babylon (Dan 9:24-27).

City of David, city of God, holy city. Rooted in God's actual dealings with his people, this theme points ahead to the fulfillment of God's promises in the coming kingdom. The city of God, then, is another way of speaking of God's kingdom.

When we think of cities in the New Testament, our minds may turn to the New Jerusalem in Revelation, or perhaps to the many cities throughout the Roman Empire where Paul and others carried the good news. In fact, both these references are related to the kingdom viewed as the city of God.

In the Sermon on the Mount, Jesus reminds his hearers that Jerusalem is "the city of the Great King" (Mt 5:35). Later Jesus wept over Jerusalem, saying, "If you, even you, had only known on this day what would bring you peace—but now it is hidden from your eyes" (Lk 19:42). In rejecting Jesus, the promised King, Jerusalem rejected the fulfillment of God's *shalom*. But the good news goes then to all peoples and cities, and the promise of the New Jerusalem remains. The New Testament, in fact, may be seen as the spreading of the good news of the kingdom throughout the cities of the Roman Empire all the way to Rome itself, leading to an expanded understanding of the city and kingdom of God. Only thus could be fulfilled the vision of the New Jerusalem filled with God's people "from every nation, tribe, people and language" (Rev 7:9).

As we would expect, the "already/not yet" tension of the kingdom cuts through the New Testament references to cities. On the one hand, the city of God is the New Jerusalem, the final coming of the kingdom, the homeland of God's people. On the other hand, the New Jerusalem has not yet come, and so God's people continue as aliens on the earth.

This picture of the church as sojourning community is sketched sharply in the epistle to the Hebrews. Abraham "was looking forward to the city with foundations, whose architect and builder is God" (Heb 11:10). God "has prepared a city" for his faithful people (Heb 11:16). We who are God's people "have come to Mount Zion, to the heavenly Jerusalem, the city of the living God" (Heb 12:22). "For here we do not have an enduring city, but we are looking for the city that is to come" (Heb 13:14).

It is clearly not the church which is this city, but rather God's kingdom. The New Testament pictures God's community (the church) within an alien community (the city), present as salt and light, as the very body of Christ, as a continuing incarnation of Jesus in the cities and kingdoms of this world. In the world, but not of it. But this is only part of the story, because God's people are absolutely sure that God is bringing his rule into the present order, and that the time is coming when the kingdoms and cities of this world shall become the very kingdom and city of God. And then city, church and kingdom will be one.

This is most magnificently pictured in Revelation 21:1-4:

Then I saw a new heaven and a new earth, for the first heaven and the first earth had passed away, and there was no longer any sea. I saw the Holy City, the new Jerusalem, coming down out of heaven from God, prepared as a bride beautifully dressed for her husband. And I heard a loud voice from the throne saying, "Now the dwelling of God is with men, and he will live with them. They will be his people, and God himself will be with them and be their God. He will wipe every tear from their eyes. There will be no more death or mourning or crying or pain, for the old order of things has passed away.

This is God's new order—a picture of the kingdom which unites and blends all the scriptural themes and illuminates God's kingdom plan. Heaven and earth have been reconciled; *shalom* has come; the garden has been restored, but now enriched through the reconciliation of God, woman and man, and all creation. So we see

the river of the water of life, as clear as crystal, flowing from the throne of God and of the Lamb down the middle of the great street of the city. On each side of the river [stands] the tree of life, bearing twelve crops of fruit, yielding its fruit every month. And the leaves of the tree are for the healing of the nations. No longer will there be any curse. The throne of God and of the Lamb will be in the city, and his servants will serve him. They will see his face, and his name will be on their foreheads. There will be no more night. They will not need the light of a lamp or the light of the sun, for the Lord God will give them light. And they will reign for ever and ever. (Rev 22:1-5)

So God's work and plan do indeed begin in a garden and end in a city—a city which is a garden, where peace and harmony reign, where all is health and ecological balance. This is the promise of the kingdom. Thus the city theme underscores another dimension of God's kingdom. The city of God is the kingdom of God.

The Narrow Gate

Visitors to Chicago often want to see the Sears Tower, so repeatedly we have made the trip downtown and up the 103 stories to the observation deck. What a view! Lake Michigan to the east; skyscrapers crowding the Loop to the north; open space, once railroad yards, to the south; and the west stretching away to the suburbs. I often think of Ellul's words, "The city is Man's greatest work." The combined beauty and strange symmetry of the city transcend any one builder's design; they speak of the total culture and creativity of humanity.

And I remember that Chicago's skyline at the 1893 World's Fair prompted Katharine Bates's hymn,

O beautiful for patriot dream
That sees beyond the years,
Thine alabaster cities gleam
Undimmed by human tears!

Kingdom people know that the dream of unstained cities is vain except as the Lord builds the city. Kingdom people look neither for a human utopia nor for a cityless, ethereal dwelling in heaven. Rather we look for the city of God. In Jesus and in the kingdom community, we "come to Mount Zion, to the heavenly Jerusalem, the city of the living God" (Heb 12:22). It is this which God promises and which he will bring.

God calls us to work with him in transforming today's urban centers into outposts of the city of God. Just as the kingdom themes of *shalom* and land are very material, this-worldly realities, so God's concern is not with "mansions in the sky" but with livable communities on earth. Finally he will bring his city and kingdom when the time comes to "restore everything" (Acts 3:21), and evil will be judged. But God's concern, and the present mission of the church, includes making the city a place of justice and peace *now*, rather than condemning and fleeing. This requires effective witness to the living Jesus Christ as both Savior and Sovereign Lord.

We must face three basic realities about cities today.

First, *cities are places of power*. They always have been, even from earliest times. The Bible itself gives us examples. Power and "the powers" concentrate in the city. Every major city is a complex of powers, whether economic, political, educational or cultural. The city is the place of power structures and of the people who run and who serve these powers. For this reason, the city is the place of the church's primary confrontation with the "principalities and powers" today.

Second, *cities are places of the poor.* The world's poor and oppressed crowd into the cities, for here they find some refuge, some basic shelter and welfare, and possibly some jobs. Meanwhile, the affluent move out to the suburbs. Large cities are like great reservoirs. A stream of humanity pours into them. The poor, the weak, the oppressed stay there, trapped in the mire at the bottom. The affluent, those rising into the middle class, move on to greener places, leaving behind the city they have used and soon forgetting the place they left behind. Thus large cities are trapped—weighed down with the growing burden of the poor, while drained of the resources of the prosperous. Businesses then follow the beautiful people, leaving behind the city's dark, stained factories for the industrial parks of the suburbs. And what about the church? Often it follows the same pattern. And so the city remains the place of the poor.

Third, *cities are places of mission.* Since cities are places of power, they are the arena of the church's witness to the principalities and powers of this world. Since cities are places of the poor, they are the field for Jesus' mission to bring the gospel to the poor. In so doing, we often *find* the gospel among the poor.

Given these realities, here are some of the things the city of God means for our churches today:

1. *We need to focus on the priority of urban mission,* both in North America and throughout the world. The earth is becoming a world of cities. Our great cities have become microcosms of the peoples, religions, ideologies and powers of the world, and they are therefore strategic for the church's mission today. Yet they are often overlooked in the evangelistic and justice witness of the church.

2. *Urban church planting and the forming of churches which visibly demonstrate reconciliation* across racial, socioeconomic and ethnic lines are a vital part of urban mission today. Our cities are places of oppression, fear and racial violence. The gospel has the *demonstrated* power to form community across such divisions (Eph 2). Today the church must imitate the first-century Christian movement in planting kingdom-style faith communities all across the urban landscape.

3. *The church is called to bring forth justice in the city,* to seek its *shalom* (Jer 29:7). We are to make the city a place of justice, especially for the poor. This means, among other things, working to elect officials who will uphold justice, not party politics; meeting physical needs through food pantries, housing rehabilitation and policy changes; and starting new businesses which provide employment, rebuild urban economies, and produce needed, ecologically sound goods and services at moderate prices.

Working for kingdom priorities in the city is the task of all Christians, not just of those who live in major cities. Every city is part of the intricate social, economic and political ecology of its region. The world, in fact, is a global network of cities. The responsibility and the opportunity to build livable cities fall on the whole church—and most pointedly on those with more than average resources and those who inhabit the wealthy green belts around our great urban centers.

The city of God is coming. Will we create urban communities which point ahead to the *shalom* of the city of God? Or will we make an interstate by-pass around this kingdom priority?

Today the way to the kingdom lies through the city, not around it. If the church's pilgrim progress by-passes the city, it may miss the kingdom.

5

Justice for the Poor

The LORD reigns forever;
he has established his throne for judgment.
He will judge the world in righteousness;
he will govern the peoples with justice.
The LORD is a refuge for the oppressed,
a stronghold in times of trouble.

Psalm 9:7-9

What does God expect of us? That we "do what is just and right. Rescue from the hand of his oppressor the one who has been robbed. Do no wrong or violence to the alien, the fatherless or the widow, and do not shed innocent blood" (Jer 22:3).

Justice for the poor is a thundering refrain throughout the Old Testament. All God's prophets speak the same language: The sovereign Lord requires justice on earth. He charges his people to be the special advocates of the poor and the oppressed.

Justice is another basic biblical theme which is being recovered today. In part, we have the stimulus of liberation theologies to thank for this. And it certainly does not further understanding or theological clarity to refer to an emphasis on this theme as "Neo-Marxist," as some evangelical missiologists have done. We are dealing here with a very prominent thread of biblical truth, not just with a current fad or secular political concept.[1]

The Old Testament is full of the concern with justice, and specifically justice for the poor and oppressed. It is woven into the fabric of Israel's Law. It is a prominent theme of Psalms, which Dietrich Bonhoeffer called the Prayer Book of Jesus. It is a key refrain in Isaiah, as well as the Minor Prophets. Isaiah says: "Stop doing wrong, learn to do right! Seek justice, encourage the oppressed" (Is 1:17). "Woe to those who . . . deprive the poor of their rights and rob my oppressed people of justice" (Is 10:1-2). God's servant "will not falter or be discouraged till he establishes justice on earth" (Is 42:4). Hear the word of the Lord:

Is not this the kind of fasting I have chosen:
to loose the chains of injustice
  and untie the cords of the yoke,
to set the oppressed free
  and break every yoke?
Is it not to share your food with the hungry
  and to provide the poor wanderer with shelter—
when you see the naked, to clothe him,
  and not to turn away from your own flesh and blood?
Then your light will break forth like the dawn,
  and your healing will quickly appear;
then your righteousness will go before you,
  and the glory of the LORD will be your rear guard.
Then you will call, and the LORD will answer;
  you will cry for help, and he will say: Here am I.
                                                    (Is 58:6-9)

As these passages show, God's particular concern is for those who are poor because of oppression. In the Old Testament, oppression is the primary cause of poverty. The Lord promises liberation and justice for the oppressed and charges his people to work justice for the poor.[2]

The kingdom thrust of this theme, however, is not merely that God's people should maintain justice for the poor, as a moral duty. It is more fundamental. God's kingdom is consistently described in the Old Testament in terms of justice for the poor and the oppressed; this is part of the basic character of the kingdom. The following are a few of the many examples of this: Psalms 10:16-18; 72:1-14; 82:1-4; 113:5-7; 146:7-10. Biblically, justice for the poor is a pivotal concern and evidence of the kingdom, both in its present reality and in its final coming.

Jesus said explicitly that he had come to preach good news to the poor (Lk 4:18; compare Mt 5:3). His life and ministry demonstrated this. He pointed to his ministry among the poor as proof of his messiahship (Lk 7:22) and said, "Blessed are you who are poor, for yours is the kingdom of God" (Lk 6:20). Jesus showed that in him God has acted decisively in behalf of the poor, and that true liberation and justice for the poor begin at the point of faith in Jesus Christ as Messiah and Lord. According to Scripture, God's people must be those who are dedicated to justice for the poor in all dimensions—spiritual, social, economic and political.

Much has been written on this subject, and there is little need to repeat it here. We may merely affirm that (1) Jesus clearly identifies himself with the Old Testament theme of justice for the poor; (2) he himself embodies this concern; (3) to seek God's kingdom and justice therefore necessarily means special concern for the poor; and (4) this concern is consistent with and reinforces the other biblical kingdom strands we have been following.

In fact, the biblical theme of justice for the poor goes to the heart of the liberating redemption God is accomplishing through Jesus Christ. God himself is just; "everything he does is right and all his ways are just" (Dan 4:37). God has shown himself "to be just and the one who justifies the [person] who has faith in Jesus" (Rom 3:26). God is both merciful and just, and through the sacrifice and victory of Jesus Christ God has proved both his mercy and justice. "The LORD has laid on him the iniquity of us all" (Is 53:6), providing the way to "justify many" (Is 53:11).

But what does it mean, really, to be justified by God through Jesus Christ? Justification, said John Wesley, "is pardon, the forgiveness of sins. It is that act of the Father whereby, for the sake of the propitiation made by the blood of his Son, he 'showeth forth his righteousness (or mercy) by the remission of sins that are past.' "[3] To be justified is to be forgiven, to be made right with God. But for what purpose? Precisely that we may live justly on earth. That, through our forgiveness and new life in Jesus, we should have the mind of Christ, walk as he walked and continue his works on earth. That we should be his body, a community of the justified who work justice. Just as Old Testament Israel was to remember their oppression in Egypt so as to be God's faithful witness-people on earth, so the church is to remember that "God chose the weak things of the world to shame the strong" (1 Cor 1:27). The church, in this sense, is "the poor" and is therefore to make justice for the poor her special love. *People who really understand what God has done for them through Jesus Christ have a special passion for justice for the poor.* They are convinced this is what it means to seek first God's kingdom and justice.

Whatever else the kingdom of God is, it is good news for the poor! This is the theme of Mary's song in Luke 1. To seek first the kingdom of God and its justice means to work justice for the poor. This is a vital and necessary sign of the kingdom.

Is the Kingdom of God Social Justice?

Picking up on the biblical theme of justice, many Christians today are showing a renewed concern for justice in society. Many are speaking of "social justice." At the same time many other Christians, at least in North America, seem deaf to this cry. But what is the meaning of "social justice"?

Jesus' followers are to seek, above all, the kingdom of God and its righteousness or justice. As I have shown elsewhere, *righteousness* in Matthew 6:33 includes the meaning of *justice;* biblically the two terms are virtually synonymous.[4] The kingdom of God is God's just rule on earth, and therefore Christians who seek first God's new order work to see justice done in every area of life. Justice, then, is a key concern of the kingdom.[5]

The fundamental meaning of *justice* in the Old Testament means both "to rule" and "to judge," so that to speak of justice in the biblical sense is already to speak of God's rule. This is significant for understanding Matthew 6:33. In Old Testament prophecy, justice and righteousness are "the means whereby the Messiah establishes the coming kingdom of peace."[6] To understand Jesus' meaning in proclaiming the kingdom, then, we must see the kingdom as the coming to earth of God's justice/righteousness through the life, ministry and ongoing rule of Jesus.

What does it mean to speak of "social" justice? Is there any other kind? Justice means relationship; justice *is* social. No one is just in a vacuum or on top of a mountain. To be righteous is to be in right relation. To be just is to treat others justly, in a way that expresses the truth about the other, a person created in God's image. God is right and just in himself precisely because he always maintains a right and just relationship with his creation. As Trinity, God is a triunity in which justice and righteousness define the interrelationships of Father, Son and Holy Spirit. And since the deepest character of God is holy love, so the deepest character of God's own intercommunity, and of all justice on earth, is love. There is no true love without justice, nor real justice without love. If we love, we act justly. And in acting justly, we demonstrate the integrity of our love. Justice is love in action.

So justice is by definition social. It is relational. To justify two objects is to line them up with each other. To justify a margin is to bring all the lines into the same relationship with each other. Justice always implies plurality, never an isolated individual.[7]

Justice is social. And since the gospel and the kingdom are all about justice, it follows that authentic Christians have an overriding concern: Justice at every level of social relationships! Since love and justice are social, Christians (who are social beings) are committed to right relationships between themselves and God, among themselves in the Christian community, and in every area of society—"to the ends of the earth."

It should be crystal clear, then, that social justice is never an option for the church. Not even the tiniest foundation stone, in theory or practice, can be found in Scripture for a wall between individual justice and social justice. The only distinction concerns the specific persons or groups where justice operates. Justice—first of all within the Godhead, then between God and his creation, then throughout the human family and in humanity's relationship with the earth. This is the heart of the kingdom. It underlies the work of evangelism as well as every other kind of witness.

The church is the people of the kingdom of justice, those who, having been justified by grace through faith, live and work to be examples and agents of justice in the Christian community and in the world.

The purpose of the kingdom is justice, and justice is social. In other words, the purpose of the kingdom is God's just, loving rule over all creation, bringing forth a world of harmony and beauty that truly glorifies God. This is the "new heaven and new earth" where justice reigns.

Justice for the poor, then, is central because of who God is. It is an expression of God's character in relation to human society. Acting justly toward the poor is simply an extension or application of justice in a more fundamental sense. This is clear when we note that all the biblical themes traced so far link with justice.

Something within us craves justice. Many lives are scarred and personalities warped because of unjust treatment received as children. This grieves the heart of God. God desires truth and justice in the deepest parts, and when we fail to act justly—in other words, when we fail to treat other people with the deep human respect they deserve because they are God-imaged persons—we both affront and grieve our Lord.

The biblical concern for justice shows us that justice between persons, communities, races and nations is all part of one picture. We are to have the same concern for justice in economic and political relationships as in our families, for we are, in fact, all part of one human family. Justice, mercy and truth call us to settle squabbles both at home and among nations.

The Narrow Gate

Jesus said in the Sermon on the Mount, "Blessed are the poor in spirit, for theirs is the kingdom of heaven" (Mt 5:3). The kingdom belongs especially to those who come to God in utter need and dependency, casting themselves in hope on God's mercy. Thus Jesus announces the reign of God, and thus the kingdom comes.

What does this mean for the church today? I would give three examples which suggest where kingdom priorities lie.

1. *Christians are called to meet the needs of the poor within the church,* following the New Testament example (Acts 4:34-35; 24:17; Rom 15:26; 2 Cor 8; Gal 2:10). The principle, says the apostle Paul, is "that there might be equality" among God's people, the plenty of some supplying the needs of others (2 Cor 8:13-14).

Forget for a moment the poor outside the church. What about needy and starving Christians *within* the body of Christ, whether in Haiti, Central Africa or Chicago? God's Word is plain here. Affluent Christians are not kingdom people if they feed and clothe themselves while ignoring their own brothers and sisters in the faith—*their own flesh and blood* in Jesus' body. This must start, of course, within each local congregation. But Christians who are sensitive at this point will not stop here. Their compassion will reach to *all* the poor, including those who do not yet know Jesus Christ. Anything less violates the justice of the kingdom and contradicts the Incarnation. It is violence and oppression.

2. *Kingdom Christians will work for justice in government policies which affect the poor,* whether on the domestic or the world scene. Christians must clearly be on the side of a just world order. Their

support of candidates for public office and for specific legislation should reflect this. This means working to dismantle the structures of oppression in our own nation (for example, inadequate pay for women and minorities) and abroad (for example, apartheid in South Africa). It means working for policies which will build families and protect human life, both of the unborn and of those born into poverty.

3. *Kingdom Christians must proclaim Jesus Christ as Savior and Liberator of the poor and oppressed.* Jesus Christ is the way to the kingdom. The oppressed need above all else to know Jesus Christ as Savior. True liberation begins as those who hunger and thirst for righteousness are filled through faith and forgiveness in Jesus Christ.

It will not do for white middle-class Christians to evangelize only people like themselves. This violates the kingdom and is a form of violence against the poor. We are called today, as surely as Jesus was, to preach and demonstrate the gospel among the poor. Evangelizing the poor—from a kingdom perspective, not just from a church perspective—is the highest priority of the church's ministry in the world.

I remember how painful it was, after several years in interracial Brazil, to return to the United States and face again the stark separation between Black and White, especially in the church. How beautiful, and how kingdomlike, to see the blending of races and classes in the Christian community, and how painful to feel the racism which simmers just below the surface among so many of us who call ourselves Christians.

This is but one example, but it reminds us of the injustice woven into society, and of how far we have to go to be kingdom people.

God's kingdom is all about justice, and especially justice for the poor and oppressed.

6

The Age of Sabbath

*By the seventh day God had finished the work
he had been doing; so on the seventh day
he rested from all his work. And God blessed
the seventh day and made it holy, because
on it he rested from all the work of creating
that he had done.*

Genesis 2:2-3

The Sabbath, so prominent in the Old Testament, is powerful kingdom truth. It derives from God's sovereignty and points toward the final age of rest when God rules without rivals. So Sabbath is closely woven with the other themes we have been noting.

Sabbath goes to the root of Israel's self-identity as a people. It begins not at Mount Sinai but at creation: "By the seventh day God had finished the work he had been doing; so on the seventh day he rested from all his work. And God blessed the seventh day and made it holy, because on it he rested from all the work of creating that he had done" (Gen 2:2-3).

Some translations mask the force of what Genesis 2:2 actually says. The Revised Standard Version is literally accurate: "On the seventh day God finished his work which he had done." Did God finish the work of creating on the sixth day or on the seventh? The original account says God finished his work on the seventh day. Why? Because God did create something on the seventh day: He created Sabbath. The Sabbath is not a negation—merely the cessation of work—but an affirmation, the creation of rest, peace, *shalom*. On the seventh day God created *shalom*—the crown and goal of all his work.

In God's rhythm, life always looks ahead to Sabbath. Life moves toward the time of peace and rest, of fulfilled meaning. For God's people, every week leads to the Sabbath climax, and all history leads to the *shalom* of the kingdom—the final, perfect Sabbath. This is the drama of the kingdom.

So it is that the Sabbath law, as part of the Mosaic covenant, is to be understood. Israel viewed the Sabbath as the heart of the law.[1] It was a day of rest, to be kept holy.

In Old Testament summaries of the law, more space is given to the Sabbath than to any other of the Ten Commandments. An interesting difference, however, appears in the two accounts of the Ten Commandments (Ex 20:1-17; Deut 5:6-21). The Sabbath law is the same in both, but the basis is different. In the Exodus account, Israel is to observe Sabbath because on the seventh day God rested, blessed and set apart that day. But Deuteronomy cites another reason: "Remember that you were slaves in Egypt and that the LORD your God brought you out of there with a mighty hand and an outstretched arm. Therefore the LORD your God has commanded you to observe the Sabbath day" (Deut 5:15).

Thus the Sabbath is grounded in both creation and in liberation or redemption. God's people have double reason to rest and remember God's covenant. They are God's people both by creation and by liberation. The same God who created the world, history and Sabbath is the God who recreates, who redeems and liberates. God is acting in the struggles of history, redeeming and preparing a people of his own, leading to the final Sabbath of the kingdom. The Sabbath becomes a sign of the faithfulness (or a testimony against the unfaithfulness) of God's covenant people. So God says, "You must observe my Sabbaths. This will be a sign between me and you for the generations to come, so you may know that I am the LORD, who makes you holy. . . . The Israelites are to observe the Sabbath, celebrating it for the generations to come as a lasting covenant. It will be a sign between me and the Israelites forever, for in six days the LORD made the heavens and the earth, and on the seventh day he abstained from work and rested" (Ex 31:13-17).

Abraham Heschel describes the Sabbath as the sanctification of time. The Hebrew faith, he says, "is *a religion of time* aiming at *the sanctification of time.*"[2] Hebrew faith is more interested in time than in space; it hallows history more than geography.[3] Heschel notes,

> To Israel the unique events of historic time were spiritually more significant than the repetitive processes in the cycle of nature, even though physical sustenance depended on the latter. While the deities of other peoples were associated with places or things, the God of Israel was the God of events: the Redeemer from slavery, the Revealer of the Torah, manifesting Himself in events of history rather than in things or places.[4]

This is not to downplay the world of space and things, but rather to put the material world in perspective. Specifically, the Sabbath puts the created world in the perspective of God's historic kingdom plan: What exists is grounded in God's creation and his plan of redemption. Things have meaning as they are seen in the flow of God's economy. As in a good mystery, the conclusion gives meaning to the flow of details, some seemingly pointless, that precede. The Sabbath is a taste of eternity.

As a kingdom theme, the Sabbath shows that God is the God of time and history. This underscores the historical character of his reign. God's kingdom is an everlasting kingdom, but not a timeless one. Time does not end in an eternal, timeless realm.

The kingdom is not timelessness, but timefulness—the fullness of time, the everlasting reign of God. The kingdom is dynamic, not static—as dynamic as the God who creates, sustains and liberates.[5]

Given the Sabbath's prominence in the Old Testament, its seemingly minor role in the New Testament may surprise us. Most of the references in the Gospels, in fact, are to charges that Jesus violated the Sabbath by healings or other "profane" activities on the sacred day. Is there any kingdom message here?

Two things immediately stand out when we look at Jesus' attitude toward the Sabbath. First, Jesus observed the Sabbath but refused to let Sabbath traditions keep him from doing the work of the kingdom. Second, Jesus said he came not to abolish the law but to fulfill it (Mt 5:17-18). He showed what this means for the Sabbath when he said, "The Sabbath was made for man, not man for the Sabbath. So the Son of Man is Lord even of the Sabbath" (Mk 2:27-28).

Thus Jesus himself is the fulfillment of the Sabbath. Sabbath finds its meaning in him—his person, work and reign—just as the kingdom centers in him. The fulfillment of the Sabbath in Jesus is symbolized by the church's adoption of the first day of the week (the day of resurrection) as her principal day of worship rather than the seventh day.

This meaning of Sabbath is expanded in Hebrews 4. Sabbath was not fulfilled when Israel entered the Promised Land. "There remains, then, a Sabbath-rest for the people of God; for anyone who enters God's rest also rests from his own work, just as God did from his. Let us, therefore, make every effort to enter that rest, so that no one will fall by following their example of disobedience" (Heb 4:9-11). The writer uses the Sabbath theme to hold out hope for a more perfect rest and to urge diligence now so we may enter God's rest.

This "rest" has often been taken to mean heaven, as in Baxter's classic _The Saints' Everlasting Rest._ But what is heaven, if not the final establishment of the kingdom of God? Hebrews pictures

Jesus as our pioneer who has gone before us, conquering sin and entering the very presence of God where "he always lives to intercede for" us (Heb 7:25). Jesus is King of Salem *(shalom)*, King of Peace (Heb 7:1-2). In him the kingdom has come in power, and through him the kingdom will come in fullness. God's people now experience Sabbath—the peace and rest found in reconciliation with God, and with sisters and brothers in the Christian community. And this very Sabbath experience gives them strength to trust and to struggle for the final kingdom rest which Jesus has assured us is coming. It is this final triumph which is pictured so graphically in the book of Revelation.

Notice that this final rest is not merely the end of conflict. It is restoration, reconciliation, liberation. It is truly the creation of Sabbath! It is God's people, and with them the whole creation, "liberated" from "bondage to decay" (Rom 8:21). Peter stresses this when he speaks of the promised "time . . . for God to restore everything" (Acts 3:21) and of the new heaven and new earth for which we yearn (2 Pet 3:13). The kingdom as God's Sabbath is perfect restoration, God's final *shalom.*

In the New Testament, then, the coming of Jesus is the decisive step toward the fulfillment of Israel's Sabbath. Jesus fulfills the law and inaugurates the kingdom. God's rest has now been internalized in a new way, with the forgiveness of sins and the indwelling of the Holy Spirit. And it has been universalized through the spread of the good news of the kingdom to all peoples, the whole earth, and the beginning reconciliation which this brings. Yet, even so, "there remains . . . a Sabbath-rest for the people of God" (Heb 4:9), for the kingdom has not yet come in its fullness. We must still "make every effort to enter that rest" (Heb 4:11); we must still seek first the kingdom of God.

The Sabbath theme thus expands and reinforces the understanding of God's kingdom revealed by other themes.

The Narrow Gate

I was brought up strictly to observe Sunday as the Sabbath. It was a special day and I felt it. It was not a day for buying and selling, business or schoolwork, but for worship and rest. Even recreational sports were frowned on. The time was hallowed. (And I found, incidentally, that six days weekly were enough to get schoolwork done, even in graduate school!)

While my ideas of Sabbath have changed some, I appreciate that training, that sense of a special day, which still remains with me. With the invasion of television and growing affluence, many North American Christians have lost all sense of Sabbath and the hallowing of time.

But Sabbath has come to have a deeper sense the more I meditate on the kingdom. There remains a Sabbath rest for God's people, and its name is the kingdom of God. What a significant step toward the kingdom, if all God's people would dedicate the Lord's Day to learning, meditating on and witnessing to the kingdom of God, the Sabbath of the Lord! How powerful for the kingdom and for kingdom living throughout the week, if we would really hallow the Sabbath day as a time for equipping God's people to be the community of the King through worship, witness and community!

Sabbath sensitivity might have several practical implications for the church today:

1. *The church should affirm the rhythm of the seven-day week, and of Sunday as a special day.* I speak here not of a new legalism, but of a new realism. God has made us part of the rhythm of nature, which reflects the truth of his own character (Gen 2:1-2). We ignore this rhythm to our own hurt; to live in harmony with it is health. The weekly Sabbath is a day of rest for body, mind and spirit, and for renewing our vision for the ultimate rest and *shalom* of the kingdom.

Part of our discipling, then, should concern our good stewardship of time, built around the weekly pattern, kingdom priorities and the sense of walking in harmony with God's reconciling work in bringing his kingdom. How will it be possible for us to see clearly what God is bringing in the future if we do not pace our lives to see and feel what he is doing now?

2. *The church needs a clearer focus on worship as a window on the kingdom.* The whole week takes its meaning from our communal worship of God, just as history takes its meaning from the reality and certainty of final kingdom Sabbath. Living a life of worship means learning the life of worship in our times of gathered praise to God. As a discipling priority, this means building our lives around the priority of weekly worship as empowerment for daily witness.

3. *Through the rhythm of its life, the church should foster greater kingdom expectancy.* What, after all, are we living for? Jesus said the kingdom must have top priority (Mt 6:33). Worship should focus not only on who God is and what he has done, but on what he is doing and promises in his kingdom plan. The worshiping, nurturing and witnessing life of the church should all be lived out in expectancy of God's final Sabbath. Sunday worship then becomes the foretaste of the coming kingdom.

In kingdom perspective, it makes sense not to build up treasures on earth, but to invest our time and resources in the work of the kingdom. Time will finally reveal the wisdom of the investment when God brings to fulfillment all his kingdom promises. How foolish it will look, then, to have gained much for ourselves but little for the kingdom!

7

The Age of Jubilee

Count off seven sabbaths of years—seven times
seven years—so that the seven sabbaths of
years amount to a period of forty-nine years.
Then have the trumpet sounded everywhere on
the tenth day of the seventh month; on the
Day of Atonement sound the trumpet throughout
your land. Consecrate the fiftieth year and
proclaim liberty throughout the land to all its
inhabitants. It shall be a jubilee for you;
each one of you is to return to his family property
and each to his own clan.
Leviticus 25:8-10

Most fascinating of all the biblical kingdom themes is the Jubilee.

The Jubilee appears first in Leviticus 25 and later is developed prophetically, especially in Isaiah 58 and 61.[1] It is based on the fact that God as King is owner of the land, and his people are stewards.

The Jubilee is a Sabbath of Sabbaths. It extends the provision of the sabbatical year by requiring all land to be returned to its original occupants. Thus the four main provisions of the Jubilee were (1) the land was to lie fallow; (2) slaves were to be liberated; (3) debts were to be cancelled; and (4) all land acquired during the forty-nine previous years was to be returned.

Note that these provisions are all fundamentally economic and ecological. Despite the various interpretations of the Jubilee, five implications, at least, are clear, and all have kingdom significance: (1) In the Jubilee, spiritual, social, economic, liturgical and historical dimensions are all interwoven. (2) The Jubilee is especially directed toward the interests of the poor, the disadvantaged and the oppressed. (3) The Jubilee is rooted in God's character as seen in creation and redemption (as evidenced, for example, in Gen 2:2-3; Ex 20; Deut 5). (4) The Jubilee concerns the relationship of God's people to God's land and is thus earthly and ecological. (5) The Jubilee combines total dependence on God's sovereignty with human freedom, responsibility, initiative and accountability. Precisely *because* God is sovereign over his people and land, his people must act in harmony with his revealed character.

Isaiah uses the Jubilee theme as a picture of the goal of God's kingdom:

> The Spirit of the Sovereign LORD is on me,
>> because the LORD has anointed me
>> to preach good news to the poor.
> He has sent me to bind up the brokenhearted,
>> to proclaim freedom for the captives
>> and release for the prisoners,
> to proclaim the year of the LORD's favor
>> and the day of vengeance of our God,
> to comfort all who mourn,
>> and provide for those who grieve in Zion—
> to bestow on them a crown of beauty
>> instead of ashes,
> the oil of gladness
>> instead of mourning,
> and a garment of praise
>> instead of a spirit of despair. (Is 61:1-3)

Here are the nature, character and breadth of the kingdom of God in Jubilee language. And this vision in turn provides the background for Jesus' own proclamation of the kingdom.

Jesus clearly identified himself with the Jubilee in his Nazareth sermon when, reading from Isaiah 61, he said, "The Spirit of the Lord is on me, because he has anointed me to preach good news to the poor. He has sent me to proclaim freedom for the prisoners and recovery of sight for the blind, to release the oppressed, to proclaim the year of the Lord's favor," and then added, "Today this scripture is fulfilled in your hearing" (Lk 4:18-21). The "year of the Lord's favor," or "the acceptable year," scholars agree, clearly refers to the proclamation of the Jubilee year.[2] Jesus' proclamation in Nazareth may actually have occurred during the Jubilee year of A.D. 26-27.[3] As Mortimer Arias says, "Jesus came to announce the Kingdom of God and he did it in Jubilee language."[4]

What did Jesus mean by proclaiming Jubilee in Luke 4? It is indisputable that Jesus here refers to the Jubilee; the question is what he intended and what it means for us today. Interpretations vary, ranging from those of Trocmé and Yoder,[5] who see here a literal Jubilee year announcement, to views which see the "release" Jesus proclaimed as exclusively "spiritual" or eschatological. What is the truth?

As we have seen, the Jubilee is tied closely to themes of justice, the land and care for the oppressed. In the Old Testament the Jubilee is an earthly, this-worldly concern. Even in Isaiah 58 and 61, where the theme looks ahead to God's decisive Jubilee, the meaning is not necessarily "spiritualized." We cannot remove the this-worldly meaning of Jubilee from the Luke 4 passage, therefore, without solid justification. On the other hand, interpretations which see Luke 4 as the proclamation of a literal Jubilee year in Jesus' own time fail to explain adequately the Jews' reaction in Nazareth or to align this proclamation with the rest of Jesus' ministry, where the Jubilee does not seem to be prominent.

The most balanced interpretation of Jesus' Nazareth sermon I have found is given by Lesslie Newbigin in his book *Sign of the Kingdom*. Jesus' Nazareth proclamation, says Newbigin, is the proclamation of a true king in the messianic tradition. It is the function of a just ruler, a true king, to bring deliverance to the oppressed. This is an application of the Davidic strand in Old Testament teaching about the Kingdom. And the reasons for which Jesus' words were rejected is not (as far as this pericope is concerned) because he was on the side of the poor against the rich. The reasons are twofold. In the first place, he offended against nationalist sentiment (verses 23-27). The suggestion that God's first care might not be Israel but the Gentiles was the first thing that aroused the popular fury against him. In the second place they took offence at his person. "Is not this Joseph's son?" they said. And so the rejection at Nazareth was not an action of "the Establishment"; the story seems to make it quite clear that it was a "people's movement" that tried to destroy him at the outset.[6]

Newbigin notes that the Gospels do indeed "carry forward the Old Testament faith that 'God has a bias in favour of the poor,' " but this must be understood "in the framework of the basic Old Testament conviction that Yahweh is the true king who intervenes to establish the cause of the oppressed against their oppressors." Thus "the cause of stumbling is that [God's] intervention is embodied in the person of this man Jesus, who does not conform to the popular expectations of the Messiah. . . . The cause of stumbling is the Person of Jesus himself."[7]

Jesus does not seem to have been inaugurating a Jubilee year. Rather he was announcing the Jubilee *age*—the very kingdom of God (Mt 4:17). But his announcement was no mere spiritual or symbolic one. Jesus healed the sick, freed the demon-possessed and gave sight to the blind—not just in a spiritual sense but physically as well. When Jesus touched the deaf and the blind they heard and saw with their *physical* ears and eyes. They were not just spiritually enlightened. Jesus is the Messiah who brings the literal fulfillment of the Jubilee provisions for justice. Thus Jesus' healings, while certainly in a sense parables of the kingdom, are not to be understood or interpreted only as illustrations of a "higher" spiritual truth (for example, of Jesus' power to open our eyes spiritually). Jesus' literal, historical healings, like his resurrection, are signs of the literal, historical character and inbreaking of the new order of God's kingdom. Thus also Jubilee is not spiritualized, nor its force blunted, by this interpretation.

Jubilee in Matthew

Luke 4, however, is not the only Jubilee passage in the New Testament. Scholars have noted the Jubilee tone of the Lord's Prayer, especially in the petition "Forgive us our debts, as we also have forgiven our debtors" (Mt 6:12; Lk 11:4),[8] and also the echoes of Isaiah 61:1-2 in the Beatitudes of Matthew 5:3-6.[9] Jesus' Sermon on the Mount (Mt 5—7) is, in fact, a Jubilee proclamation, functioning in Matthew much as the Nazareth discourse does in Luke. Fundamentally and thematically, Jesus in the Sermon on the Mount fulfills the prophecy of Isaiah 61, just as he did (more explicitly but less fully) in the Nazareth synagogue. The Sermon on the Mount announces Jubilee. Here the present kingdom meaning of Jubilee is set forth. To announce the kingdom is to proclaim "the favorable year of the Lord."

The Sermon on the Mount (especially the Beatitudes) stands in the same relation to the Old Testament Jubilee theme as it does to the Old Testament law (the Old Covenant) generally. On the one hand, the Old Testament Jubilee material reveals God's *character* and *intention* for his people for all time, including New Testament times; on the other hand, Jesus' words show what the Jubilee means concretely *now*, in the New Covenant, and in the kingdom of God, present and future.

A comparison of Matthew 5:3-10 with Isaiah 61:1-2 and Psalm 146:7-8 shows clearly, I think, the Jubilee character of the Beatitudes. Isaiah 61:1-2 depicts the Messiah preaching good news to the poor, the basic and introductory act in his appearance—and this is precisely what Jesus does. He begins to preach to the crowds, and his first words are about the poor, fulfilling the Isaiah prophecy.

Jubilee and Kingdom

The mystery and the stumbling block, of course, are that the kingdom did not suddenly spring into fullness immediately. This is a basic mystery of the kingdom. The answer, however, is not that Jesus intended a spiritual rather than a literal, material coming of the kingdom. That suggestion is a cop-out. The answer is rather the question of *how God chooses to bring in his kingdom.* The kingdom centers in Jesus, and the coming of the kingdom in its fullness on earth still hinges on faith in Jesus and obedience to his word. There is no other way. In Jesus, and in the full coming of his kingdom, God has chosen first of all the power of powerlessness. The kingdom comes through suffering, servanthood and much that the wisdom of this world calls foolishness (1 Cor 1:20—2:7).

But the kingdom finally will come in power, and even in wrath toward all untruth and injustice. The book of Revelation leaves no doubt about that. Revelation 11:15-19, for example, pictures this climax, when "the kingdom of the world" becomes "the kingdom of our Lord and of his Christ" (Rev 11:15). This prophecy ties in with the Jubilee and with the land, for God's victory is announced at the blowing of the seventh trumpet (probably a Jubilee motif).[10] God is praised for taking his "great power" and beginning to reign (Rev 11:17). The time for judgment has come, "and for destroying those who destroy the earth" or land (Rev 11:18). So the coming of the kingdom is the coming of the final Jubilee and the deliverance of the earth from all oppression and alienation.

Nothing in the New Testament cancels the breadth, literalness or ecological character of the Old Testament Jubilee theme. God still will bring the Jubilee, the Sabbath of Sabbaths. The New Testament makes clear, however, that the Jubilee comes solely through Jesus Christ. For the church today, the Jubilee theme can serve "as a paradigm of Kingdom action in the world," as Mortimer Arias says, assisting us "to develop a missionary vision and model in the Kingdom perspective."[11]

The Narrow Gate

What does this mean practically? How can the church more intentionally demonstrate the meaning of Jubilee in the world today?

Here are some examples:

1. *Jesus Christ can be presented as the one who brings Jubilee, the liberator from bondage.* Starting with the New Testament, but rooted in the Old, we can lift up Jesus as the Messiah who opens the door to the real Jubilee of the kingdom. This begins with proclaiming and serving the Jesus who comes not only to justify sinners before God but to form a just community which demonstrates Jubilee liberation in the world. If faithful to Jesus' Jubilee message, the church will present Jesus as the one who liberates the oppressed from bondage and who brings final Jubilee in the fullness of the revelation of the kingdom.

2. *The Jubilee gospel focuses on the gospel for the poor.* Jesus makes this unmistakably plain, as we have seen (Mt 5:3-10; 11:5, 28; 25:40; Lk 4:18; 6:20; 7:22; 14:13, 21). He fulfills in himself and in his body the prophetic promises of a Messiah who comes to bring justice for the poor and oppressed.

A church infected with kingdom passion will be the presence of Jesus among the poor. It will present Jesus as Savior from sin, Liberator from the bondages of spirit and body, and Ruler who prepares us to welcome his reign. With power and without apology such a church will evangelize among the poor, inviting women and men to experience the new birth and the new life of Christian community. It will disciple converts to become servants and ministers of Jesus Christ in the world. It will build communities of believers whose character is Jubilee.

3. *Jubilee means demonstrated commitment to economic justice in society.* This was the central provision of the ancient Jubilee law, and it continues today because the gospel concerns koinonia—how people share the resources of life God has given us.

This liberation begins in the church, as noted in earlier chapters, as Christians work justice for all believing sisters and brothers. But it also means siding with efforts for economic justice in society. The church cannot justly claim Jesus for its own unless it follows him "outside the gate" (Heb 13:12 RSV).

How can the church work Jubilee justice here and now in anticipation of the final kingdom? This will depend on the places of injustice around us, in the neighborhood and around the world. It will mean finding working ways to relieve the poor from bondage, not only through evangelism but also through finding cures for institutionalized injustice. Real Jubilee is not just relief for victims, but structural change to bring justice (Lev 25). Out of their own sense of freedom from sin through Jesus Christ, Jubilee Christians work to eliminate the evil institutionalized in such places as unfair employment practices, discrimination in housing and barriers to providing help to the world's poor. One Jubilee action, for example, might be working to change government policies which reward farmers for not growing food while millions starve in other lands.

The Bible allows no either/or on the Jubilee theme. We take nothing away from the final, full, eschatological meaning of Jubilee when we also stress its present relevance. Rather, in pressing for Jubilee *now*, we are faithful to the gospel and even now spread the leaven of the kingdom.

Conclusion: Seven Themes, One Kingdom

In tracing the biblical themes of peace, land, house, city, justice, Sabbath and Jubilee, we have seen that all are wrapped up with God's kingdom. These seven themes show that the kingdom is much broader, much more profound, than it may at first appear.

In the Old Testament, these themes reveal the character of the kingdom. The kingdom is God's rule actually manifested on earth, based on God's total sovereignty and mighty acts, and including a covenant relationship with God's people whereby they bind themselves to live consistently with God's revealed character. Woven together, these themes provide a comprehensive foundation for the biblical vision of God's kingdom.

John Perkins nicely shows how several of these themes combine when viewed from the perspective of justice, "the highest form of love." Justice in this sense, he says, "means (1) to recognize God as the Creator and owner of the earth, (2) to allow man to scratch into the earth with his own hands and enjoy the fruit of his labor, and (3) to be able to raise one's hands in the praise of God. Justice is to have a sabbath."[12]

The message of the New Testament is that the kingdom has drawn near and become visible in Jesus Christ. This is the "mystery" or "secret" of the kingdom. With the Incarnation, the kingdom is embodied in Jesus—though not unambiguously and not yet in its fullness. Jesus is the King and the agent of the kingdom. And he is now present and reigning through the Holy Spirit who is the foretaste and firstfruit of the church's kingdom witness. The presence of the Spirit, as Lesslie Newbigin has said, "is not the lantern which a traveller in the dark carries in his hand; it is the glow on his face which reflects the coming dawn."[13]

The kingdom centers, above all, in Jesus Christ—the one who has "disarmed the powers and authorities, . . . triumphing over them by the cross" (Col 2:15), who has been raised "far above all rule and authority, power and dominion, and every title that can be given, not only in the present age but also in the one to come" (Eph 1:21). Wherever Jesus is, there the kingdom is. Wherever Jesus Christ is working, there the new order is breaking in. Wherever Jesus is working among the poor, there the prophecies that God will bring justice for the poor have their initial fulfillment.

We may summarize the New Testament treatment of these seven kingdom themes by saying that in the New Testament these themes are both *internalized* and *universalized*. Their *inward* thrust is intensified while their *outward* thrust is expanded. To be more precise, in the New Testament we find these themes (1) internalized but not merely spiritualized; (2) universalized but not merely symbolized; (3) partially but not fully realized; and (4) their eschatological focus is clarified but still not fully revealed.

The mystery is dramatically opened and illustrated, but in a way that still leaves us guessing. We are left in awe, for the more we understand, the greater we see is the mystery yet to be revealed.[14]

The New Testament weaves these seven themes together to form a consistent, strong theology of the kingdom. Each theme points to Jesus Christ, the person of the kingdom, through whom God's kingdom promises are fulfilled. Jesus is the Prince of Peace, the one who brings justice for the poor, the true builder of the city of God. He promises and brings Sabbath rest, both now and in final Jubilee fullness. And he is the one who redeems his land, his earth, in God's kingdom economy to unite all things in himself and free the whole created order from its bondage to decay.

Have we seen the kingdom? Are we living the kingdom? Is it for us precisely what Jesus said it should be—our highest and greatest quest?

Part Two
The Present Challenge

8

The People of the Kingdom

Bob Pierce was a Christian giant of our time. Evangelist, pioneer Youth for Christ worker, and prophetic founder of World Vision, he helped turn conservative North American Protestants outward to the social implications of the gospel. Yet, as his daughter's tender biography of this evangelical prophet frankly shows, Pierce's life was one of conflict, strained relationships and near tragedy.[1]

Here was a man who gave himself fully for homeless Korean War orphans but often sacrificed his own family. He had a vision from God, but he was never adequately discipled, never so immersed in an accountable community of believers that he could be both supported and disciplined so that life and ministry were one.

Unfortunately, this story is all too common in the church. Bob Pierce's life is a vivid lesson of what happens when kingdom ministry is divorced from kingdom community.

The forties and fifties in the United States brought forth a host of new evangelical ministries, many with worldwide impact. God has used these to expand the church's witness. Yet often our witness has been flawed from lack of understanding that the work of the kingdom must be grounded in the community of the King.

Whatever their weaknesses and failures, the first Christians were kingdom people, a community of the King. They continued the very works of Jesus, their Lord, in the spirit of Isaiah 61. They cared not only for their own, but for thousands of the poor around them. And they did so, like the Jerusalem Christians in Acts 2—5, out of the overflow of life together in Christian community. About A.D. 125 the Christian philosopher Aristides wrote,

> They walk in all humility and kindness, and falsehood is not found among them. They love one another. They despise not the widow, and grieve not the orphan. Whoever has distributes liberally to whoever has not. If they see a stranger, they bring him under their roof, and rejoice over him as if he were their own brother: for they call themselves brothers, not after the flesh, but after the Spirit of God. When one of their poor passes away from the world, and any of them see him, then he provides for his burial according to his ability; and if they hear that any of their number is imprisoned or oppressed for the name of their Messiah, all of them provide for his needs, and if it is possible that he may be delivered, they deliver him. And if there is among them a man that is poor and needy, and they have not an abundance of necessities, they fast two or three days that they may supply the needy with their necessary food.[2]

The church is the *body* of Christ. In a very real sense, the church is not only a sign but also (when faithful to Christ and led by the Spirit) the agent of the kingdom on earth. The church is not the kingdom; neither is it unrelated to the kingdom. It is the witness to the kingdom and, when anointed and animated by the Holy Spirit, becomes in a partial though not unambiguous way the sign, prototype and pilot project of the kingdom on earth.

E. Stanley Jones has expressed well this dynamic, sometimes paradoxical tie between church and kingdom:

> Christ loved the Church and gave Himself for it that He might

redeem it. But he never gave Himself for the Kingdom to redeem it. For the Kingdom is itself redemption. It is not the subject of redemption—it offers it. The difference is profound. The Church may be, and is, the agent of the coming of that redemption, but it is the agent and not the Absolute. I am bound to be loyal to the Church to the degree that it is loyal to the Kingdom, but my highest loyalty is to the Kingdom, and when these loyalties conflict, then I must bow the knee finally to the Kingdom. Any false loyalty to the Church which would make it take the place of the Kingdom is destructive to the Church.[3]

Yet Jesus does, in fact, choose to use the church. Whenever Jesus is actually working through his body, there the church is an authentic sign of the kingdom. And if the church as a literal, space-time community is really the *body*—the embodiment, the infleshment—of Jesus Christ, it is not too much to say that the church, headed by Christ and animated by the Spirit, is the *agent* of the kingdom on earth in the present order (though not the sole agent; God also works outside and beyond the church).[4] *The church is the primary point of entry of the new order of the kingdom into present history.* It is salt and light, a city on a hill. It is not the kingdom, and at times may actually betray the kingdom, but is nevertheless in a fundamental way the sacrament and sign of the kingdom in today's world.

The Kingdom Community

Here is both the church's high calling and her constant challenge and possibility. Yet how frequently believers misunderstand and underexperience the church as kingdom community.

The church is called to be both redemptively present in the world and yet separated from bondage to the world's values. Here we can learn from the sixteenth-century Anabaptists. As Harold Bender notes, these radical reformers gave witness to committed community and personal integrity for several basic reasons:

(1) They insisted upon personal conviction, conversion, and

commitment as adults, based upon prior teaching. (2) They made the above a requirement for admission to church membership. (3) They worshiped mostly in small groups with intimacy of personal acquaintance, testimony, observation, and admonition. (4) They practiced church discipline. (5) They had high standards for the Christian life, which were so much higher than the average of the society of the time that only really committed persons would accept them and seek to fulfill them. (6) They practiced separation from the world and so were delivered from the constant influence of the low-living multitude.[5]

The challenge before us today is to be radically committed to Jesus and his reign and, precisely for that reason, to be radically committed to the world God has made. This is possible in only one way: *through radical commitment to one another in the body of Christ.* Christians must understand and experience the reality that in the church believers *really are* members of one another.[6]

This raises two questions: How we understand the church biblically, and how we live our lives together in Christian community according to kingdom principles. I have discussed the nature of the church at length elsewhere,[7] and in the last chapter of this book will propose several kingdom operating principles. Here I would like to examine briefly the thorny question of how the church can successfully hold together the present and the future, inward and outward, personal and social, spiritual and secular dimensions of our communal life as Christians.

While this question has some theoretical answers, I believe its primary solution lies in the *practice* of the church's life together. The answer is to be found in really living as a kingdom community, where the worship, community and witness of the church are all rooted in the reality that the church exists under the sovereign reign of Christ.

The reality of the kingdom gives the church both an overarching theological framework for its life and also practical handles for holding the various dimensions of the kingdom creatively together. The kingdom tells us that God is the God of "all things in heaven and on earth" (Eph 1:10), and that, in God's kingdom plan, all dimensions of reality are in fact part of one total web.

The interrelatedness of all aspects of creation under God's sovereignty is in fact one of the central truths of the kingdom. We have trouble keeping a balance among the various aspects of the biblical gospel in part because we often lack a sufficiently biblical kingdom theology.

The difficulty of maintaining a kingdom balance is perhaps nowhere more evident than in the relationship between the priorities of evangelism and justice. How can the church, in practice, maintain a biblical balance here?

Rather than giving a theoretical answer, let me suggest a visual model which integrates these two concerns by tying them to the kingdom and to discipleship (see figure 1).

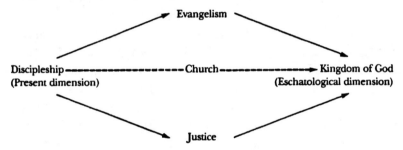

Figure 1.

The kingdom of God provides the eschatological focus of the church (not only as *future*, but also as *the future present*), giving direction and purpose to the church's discipling ministry. This discipling ministry equips believers for their priestly service as gospel ministers (Eph 4:11-12), in part through the diversity of gifts. Discipling produces workers, ministries and structures which focus on evangelism, justice or both, depending on the Holy Spirit's choosing. In other words, discipling brings forth effective, Spirit-guided evangelism *and* social witness, both of which find their justification, focus and goal in the kingdom of God.

This is the practical answer to the common hang-up between evangelism and social action, or between the evangelistic and prophetic dimensions of the church's witness. If we understand that all genuine ministry in Jesus' name is really witness to the kingdom, we have solved the conflict conceptually. And if we disciple all believers into their God-given ministries, with a full kingdom understanding of what witness really is, we solve the conflict practically.[8]

How exciting, how liberating to be part of a faith community where some are involved in evangelism, others in servant and justice ministries, and still others in worship and discipling. In such a community, all participate in the work of the kingdom, and any conflict between evangelism and social action is clearly absurd. Evangelism is authenticated by the church's justice ministries, and becomes an invitation not only to Christ and the church, but to Jesus' kingdom work in the world.

The church, then, as a kingdom people, is to be a community of witness and justice. It is to model, even to participate in, the character of its Lord (2 Pet 1:4). If the church is authentically the kingdom community, it is a people at once renewed after the image of God, living the mind of Christ and embodying the justice of God. For in the economy of the kingdom these all mean the same thing.

This is the vision of the church as the people of the kingdom. Yet some wonder, is all this talk of the kingdom realism or mere idealism? So we must raise the question of the *possibility* of the kingdom.

9

The Possibility of the Kingdom

God's kingdom is beautiful. But is it possible? The kingdom is God's rule over all he has made. This is revealed now only partially, but will oe manifested fully with the return of Jesus Christ. Jesus brings a new heaven and new earth filled with peace, justice and love. He will set the whole creation free from its "bondage to decay" and bring it "into the glorious freedom of the children of God" (Rom 8:21), fulfilling completely all the biblical promises for an age of real *shalom* on earth.

The Possible Kingdom?

The kingdom of God, then, looks ahead to an age and environment of peace, justice and love analogous to but greater than that of the Garden of Eden, one based on just economic, political and social relationships, and ecological harmony and balance throughout the creation, with God as supreme ruler, Father and Mother (Is 66:13), and Friend of all, worshiped and glorified by the whole creation. Biblically, this is not an otherworldly, disembodied, nonmaterial, nonhistorical, spiritual realm of existence, but something sufficiently like present experience that our own bodies will be resurrected to be a part of it. Certainly we will all be changed and pass into a new dimension of existence where death and the ravages of sin will be no more. But this will come not by the total destruction of this world but by its *liberation* (Rom 8:21) through a process of death and resurrection.

Such a perspective, however, raises a fundamental question: How much of the promised new order of the kingdom is possible now? Should we expect to see the kingdom of God come *on earth*, in the present age, even before the return of Christ—if not in its fullness, at least in such a significant, anticipatory way as to bring about an age of peace, love and justice so far unprecedented in human history? Is this a legitimate hope, or is it a dangerous delusion? And on what biblical grounds do we argue the question?

In a sense the question is really unanswerable, because it depends on the sovereignty of God and the mysterious working of the Holy Spirit, and perhaps on other data beyond our knowledge. I do not find biblical support, however, either for denying the possibility of a substantial realization of the kingdom now, before Christ's return, or for spiritualizing the very material, historical, this-worldly nature of kingdom promises.

We too easily take biblical descriptions of the apostasy and moral degeneration of the last days (which after all represent only one strand of biblical truth) as reason for not placing high priority on issues of justice and peace. Yet we do not do the same in the area of evangelism and church growth!

Consistency would demand that if the future is predetermined to be an age of darkness and decline, we should give up building the church. Or else, conversely, if we are to evangelize aggressively, trusting in the work of the Holy Spirit, we should work with equal fervor for the manifestation now of the peace and justice of the kingdom, with the same trust in the Spirit. Why do we not do so? I think there is one overriding reason: We do not *really believe* that issues of justice are as important as evangelism because we have accepted an unbiblical soul-body dichotomy which says that, in the final analysis, God saves souls, not bodies.

This nonbiblical view is often made worse by an overly spiritual-psychological view of human personhood which holds that isolated individuals, distinct and separable from their social and physical environment, are really what matter. Human society and community, and therefore issues of the environment and politics and economics, are viewed as secondary concerns; they are less real, less ultimate. They are important only to the degree they affect our "spiritual life." This, however, is in flat contradiction to the biblical vision of the new order of God's kingdom. It allows for a sharper break between the present age and the age to come than Scripture does.

We have no *biblical* warrant not to work for, expect and in fact experience a much greater inbreaking of the kingdom of God now than has ever occurred in history. I would go so far as to suggest that if this is *not* our stance, we have placed our faith in something other than the promises of God himself—most likely in a particular ideology, millennial framework, or political or philosophical position which has become our key for interpreting God's promises. Yet "Abram believed the LORD" when he promised, and God "credited it to him as righteousness" (Gen 15:6).

So the real problem is a nonbiblical spirit-matter split which colors all our thinking. This produces no end of mischief, both practically and theologically. One grave result is that it permits us to abandon the whole area of economics, placing it outside the realm of central kingdom significance (which Scripture does not do).[1] Thus too often we grant economic life (and particularly, in our context, the capitalist free-enterprise system) an autonomous, amoral existence, failing to bring this area captive to kingdom priorities. It is partly for this reason that I have argued for an ecological understanding of God's plan and kingdom in my book *Liberating the Church.* From the ecological perspective, no divorce can be tolerated between the spiritual and other dimensions of existence. In God's created order everything is interrelated, and every human relationship is at once spiritual, physical, social, political and economic.

This is not to say, of course, that the present material side of human life is more important than the eternal spiritual dimension. Men and women are eternal beings, and their eternal destiny is at stake in their response to the gospel of the kingdom. The question is: How do these two dimensions connect with each other? The biblical answer, it seems to me, is not that life and history move ultimately from a material to a nonmaterial realm, but rather that material life and history are taken up into and transformed in the final climactic coming of the kingdom, and that the spiritual, eternal realm of existence *already* penetrates and permeates the present world in a mysterious way that only Christians can comprehend. Kingdom people are now, already, Paul tells us, "in the heavenly realms" (Eph 2:6). And Jesus' own incarnation and resurrection are the model here.[2]

I have tried in this book to be both biblical and realistic about the kingdom, for biblical truth is the highest and fullest realism. The kingdom of God is fact, not theory. God reigns in truth, not just as an idea. In E. Stanley Jones's words, the kingdom of God is, indeed, *realism*.

But if so, where are the visible signs of the kingdom? If Jesus Christ, head and body, is the true agent of the kingdom, where are the acts which signify the kingdom present? In particular, how does the church *in fact* either sign forth or else betray the kingdom?

Signs of the Kingdom?

The church really does sign and point toward the kingdom in more ways than most Christians realize. In rather amazing, often hidden, ways the church embryonically embodies the kingdom *now*, on earth. Here, for example, are some of these ways:

1. By being the only worldwide, transnational, multiethnic body of people seeking to love God and all humankind and confess Jesus Christ as Lord.

2. By serving as the instrument to bring many thousands of people daily to faith in Jesus Christ and into the Christian community.

3. By strengthening or rebuilding society through the creation of stable families, neighborhoods, Christian congregations and other microstructures of society.

4. By being the most effective and universal agency in the world working to meet human need, relieve suffering, and defend the cause of the poor and oppressed, giving a voice to the aspirations of the "nonpersons" of society.

5. By progressively permeating non-Christian societies (and even religions) with the moral values of the Christian revelation.

6. Through sustaining the hope and vision of a just world order based on peace, love, and mutual respect for the earth and all human beings.

7. By providing a significant check on the violent, dehumanizing tendencies of human society and helping maintain political and social stability.

8. By preserving human culture and learning through education, literature and other means.

These are some of the ways the church raises signs of the kingdom when it really is faithful to the good news as given in Scripture and in Jesus Christ. When the church effectively and authentically combines her evangelistic and prophetic witness within a vision of the kingdom, these forms of church life and ministry point to the reality of God's kingdom.

Conversely, the church often betrays the kingdom of God in the following ways:

1. By failing to demonstrate fully the unity and solidarity of the body of Christ, especially across national, racial, political and socioeconomic barriers.

2. By failing to present clearly and directly the good news of salvation through repentance and faith in Jesus Christ, winning people to new life in Jesus and in his body.

3. By mistreating and despoiling the natural environment rath-

er than working toward reconciliation between humankind and nature.

4. By supporting or undergirding oppressive political and economic structures and ideologies—especially by supporting nationalistic militarism, and exploitative economic and military intervention—and by condoning and actively supporting the oppressive role of transnational corporations in the Third World.

5. Where the church exists in circumstances of affluence, by consuming an excessive and disproportionate share of the world's energy, food and other resources.

6. By making void the Word of God through tradition, especially in the areas of the doctrine, structures and practices of the church, failing to be the Spirit-ignited community of God's people according to the biblical pattern.

7. By consuming a disproportionate share of her resources on her own comfort and maintenance.

8. By compromising the authority of Scripture, either through unbelief or through hermeneutical frameworks which are in conflict with Scripture.

9. Through overindividualizing the gospel, denying the this-worldly, material thrust of much of God's revelation and redemptive plan.

10. Through turning the church primarily into an institution rather than a sociospiritual organism, in the process denying much of the unique character and dynamic of the church.

11. Relatedly, through restricting ministry to a male-dominated clergy elite, effectively denying the priesthood of believers and the gifts of the Spirit.

Does the kingdom of God come gradually or suddenly? A little reflection should tell us that the answer is *both*. It comes mysteriously, but it comes both in shaking events and quiet changes. The kingdom, E. Stanley Jones wrote, "is coming all the time as [people] receive it, coming as silently as the dawn. It steals through the thinking and purposes of men like leaven, stirring, changing, and redeeming. . . . Jesus emphasized this gradualism, and yet He was also emphatic about the catastrophic, apocalyptic coming of the Kingdom. In this He was realistic, for, though gripped by the fact of the sudden cataclysmic coming, He did not overlook the quiet, unobtrusive coming of that Kingdom in individual acceptance and in corporate permeation."[3]

The signs and countersigns of the kingdom suggested above prove the point. When we look for signs of the kingdom, we find pluses and minuses. Yet the kingdom is coming. It is possible, and it is promised. It is also betrayed by those called to be the children of the kingdom. But the kingdom is a fact, and the fact will finally be fully revealed to all.

In the final analysis the kingdom cannot be defeated. It is God's work. Our high calling is to cooperate with what he is doing, to show in our own lives and church communities the possibility of the kingdom.

God's kingdom is still coming. Like yeast, it is still leavening. Like a seed, it is still growing, sending out shoots in every direction. Biblically, the kingdom of God is genuine potential and possibility. It is biblical realism at its most basic, grounded in the historical reality of the life, death, resurrection and continuing reign of Jesus Christ. God is doing his work, and here and there, little by little, the eyes of faith *see*.

Few people in history have seen God's power at work in society as did John Wesley. What did he think about the possibility of the kingdom? After seeing revival and reform over several decades in England, he wrote, "At the first breaking out of [God's] work in this or that place, there may be a shower, a torrent of grace; and so at some other particular seasons, which 'the Father has reserved in his own power': But in general, it seems, the kingdom of God will not 'come with observation;' but will silently increase, wherever it is set up, and spread from heart to heart, from house to house, from town to town, from one kingdom to another."[4]

Wesley went on to say that "in every nation under heaven, we may reasonably believe, God will observe the same order which he hath done from the beginning of Christianity. They shall all know me, saith the Lord;' not from the greatest to the least; (this is that wisdom of the world, which is foolishness with God;) but, 'from the least to the greatest;' that the praise may not be of men, but of God. Before the end, even the rich shall enter the kingdom of God."[5]

How the Kingdom Comes

Jesus himself shows how the kingdom comes in his master parable of the sower (Mk 4:1-20). The parable, Jesus says, concerns "the secret of the kingdom of God" (Mk 4:11). What is this secret? It has to do with the sowing, hearing and response to the Word of God. Here is the secret of how the kingdom will conquer the earth, Jesus tells us. The kingdom will come (1) through the sowing of the Word, (2) through the indifference or rejection by most people, and (3) through the fruitfulness of those who accept and continue in God's way. These will bring forth fruit "thirty, sixty or even a hundred times what was sown" (Mk 4:20). In other words, the gospel of Jesus Christ will unleash power far beyond the evil in the world. This happens not with worldly force and power, but precisely through the faithful, fruitful discipleship of God's people. Such is the secret of the kingdom, and such the key role of the church.

Not long ago in Hunan Province, China, a house-church evangelist stood before several score Chinese packed together in a secret meeting. He spoke the gospel with authority, and about one hundred gave themselves to Christ that night. Now a warrant has been posted for his arrest, charging him with "disturbing the social order" and "deceiving" four hundred people into converting to Christianity.[6]

Mainland China fell to Communism decades ago, but below the surface the yeast of the kingdom has been working. A house-church revival has spread through wide areas of China, reminiscent of the church's growth in other ages. The church has grown to thirty million or more. Cut off from Western influences, Chinese believers have rediscovered the New Testament church.

One can only imagine the kingdom impact millions of little believing communities will have in China over the next couple of generations!

Is this not another sign of the kingdom? Another evidence of its possibility and sign of its promise?

With confidence in God and hope for kingdom renewal in the church, Christians today can be agents of God's kingdom in unprecedented ways.

10
The Project of the Kingdom

History and today's news show it is fully possible for Christians to have a tremendous impact on society. But is their impact for or against the kingdom?

Since the kingdom remains a mystery, and since the long-term consequences of our actions are often unclear, we must always be cautious about any claim that our work is building God's new order. Yet certainly to seek God's kingdom and justice means working to move the world in the direction of kingdom priorities. And this is the task of the church.

The first kingdom task is to build churches which live by kingdom principles. We must be clear about this. Jesus has given us the model and example here. He proclaimed the kingdom and formed a "little flock" (Lk 12:32) to live the kingdom life. So it must be with us. Kingdom work is inviting children, women and men to Christ; nurturing those who respond in repentance, obedience and faith into kingdom living; building committed faith communities of worship, community and witness. I will speak more about this in the final chapter.

But can we be more specific about how Christians can work for kingdom priorities in their public life in society? What is the church's task, beyond evangelism? Some practical proposals need to be considered. Without setting forth a complete program or policy, I would suggest some goals Christians might work for today which could move us closer to the justice, mercy and truth of the kingdom. I will limit myself to five major areas which may be taken as paradigms, or strategic examples, of kingdom concerns in the social order: international peace and justice, militarization, economic options, foreign policy, and urbanization.

Some have suggested that I omit some of the more controversial political discussion and analysis in this section, but in good conscience I cannot do so. I offer this advice to readers: if the perspective here *really* doesn't make sense biblically, from a kingdom perspective, then dismiss it as irrelevant. But if there is biblical truth here, wrestle with it. Precisely at some of these points the kingdom easily gets betrayed by many sincere North American Christians.

1. Toward International Peace and Justice

An intriguing proposal for taming the arms race and building international peace is set forth by Bob Goudzwaard in *Idols of Our Time*. His proposal addresses the moral outrage of nations spending more on armaments than would be needed to wipe out poverty worldwide:

> Today's stress on weapons puts heavy pressure on our economies. Official figures tell us that in Europe an average of 24.4% of central government expenditures, or nearly one-fourth, goes to arms. The corresponding figure in North America is 22.6%. At the same time, government deficits have soared. . . . But suppose for a moment that a number of countries curtailed their weapons effort and cut back their weapons expenditures. In and of itself nothing positive would come of this change: unemployment would only increase. But suppose again that year by year the monies which this shift freed up were earmarked for two purposes. First, the monies would cancel the debts of the poorest countries of the world

and relieve them of their interest payments—under the condition that these countries would also decrease their weapons expenditures. Second, the monies would be used to create additional employment in our own countries. This employment would be directed at areas and people that we have abandoned: the environment, people in mental-health institutions, the quality of human labor and the inhabitability of our rotting cities. What could we expect from this move? A double measure of healing could come. First, the poorest developing countries would gradually be rid of their oppressive financial burdens and be able to grow peacefully. In *their* growth and in *their* well-being could lie *our* peace. Peaceful trade with them could flourish. Second, the United States and Europe would begin an economic *conversion*, fulfilling to some degree Isaiah's prophecy that nations "will beat their swords into plowshares and their spears into pruning hooks." The biblical image of the pruning hook suggests doing something with labor-intensive care. Conversion is possible if we do not make selfish income demands and if we pattern ourselves after an economy of care, an economy of enough.[1]

This proposal is sound both economically and ecologically. It could be politically realistic, if real moral leadership were injected into policy discussions. It fits kingdom priorities. Goudzwaard traces some of the further benefits which could result:

We have "tilled the earth," but we have systematically avoided the second half of our mandate, namely, "to take care of it." Therein lie the labor possibilities of the future. The loss caused by decreasing our weapons expenditures would return to us by way of the poorest countries and by way of conversion in our own country. If we lessen our financial demands, government deficits will decrease too. Our spirals will then start to spin in the other direction, especially in the poorest countries. If we realign our economies, then the poor countries can pursue the peaceful reconstruction of their economies. But such reconstruction will take place only if the poor countries cooperate and only if we give them the opportunity.[2]

Christians working for such policies would be seeking the priorities of the kingdom. They would be working toward international *shalom*, justice for the poor and the stewardship of God's land. A move to cancel foreign debts could be one practical application of the Jubilee principle.

We might, in fact, consider various ways to apply the Jubilee in the economic world today. In his discussion of the kingdom, Pat Robertson writes,

> I believe it is quite possible the year of jubilee will be the only way out, short of the collapse for our world in its current economic slide. The United States Government, and indeed all governments, have . . . reached the point of insupportable debt. . . . Early in the decade, the estimated worldwide debt was $10 trillion, with interest payments reaching the point where nations cannot meet them. The United States itself owed $1 trillion, and efforts to correct its economic trends set off dangerous convulsions. Notwithstanding the sneers of many in the banking community, it may be that God's way will be the only one open to us—a year of jubilee to straighten out the mess.[3]

These suggestions show both the relevance and the urgency of seeking kingdom priorities today in the international sphere.

2. Taming the Military

One of the greatest challenges facing all nations today is militarization. The problem is not merely the arms race, but the deeper issue of militarism worldwide. Growing, technologically sophisticated military establishments in dozens of nations not only increase the likelihood of war, they also divert food from the poor. It is, literally, a question of bombs or bread. And those who end up without the bread are the world's poor, those who are literally starving, not the middle-class citizens whose tax dollars pay the arms bill.

Are there ways of taming the military monster? Psychiatrist M.

Scott Peck says a major part of the problem is that we have allowed the military to become a "specialty group" which behaves according to its own rules and is practically unaccountable to the larger society. From his analysis of the My Lai massacre in Vietnam, which he helped investigate, Peck concludes, "It is not only possible but easy and even natural for a large group to commit evil without emotional involvement simply by turning loose its specialists. It happened in Vietnam. It happened in Nazi Germany. I am afraid it will happen again."[4] He sees the move to a volunteer army as increasing the danger. "Abandoning the concept of the citizen soldier in favor of the mercenary, we have placed ourselves in great jeopardy."[5]

Peck proposes transforming the military into a national service corps. He says,

As long as we must have a military organization, I suggest that our society must seriously consider de-specializing it to the ultimate degree possible. What I would propose is a combination of several old ideas: universal service and a national service corps. In place of the military as it currently exists we could have a national service corps that would perform military functions but that would also be extensively utilized for peaceful functions as well: slum clearance, environmental protection, job training education, and other vital civilian needs. Instead of the corps being an all-volunteer force or being fed by some inequitable draft system, it could be based on a system of obligatory national service for all American youth, male and female. They would not be conscripted for cannon fodder but would be employed for a whole variety of necessary tasks. The requirement for all youth to serve would at one and the same time make military adventurism more difficult but would facilitate full-scale mobilization if necessary. Having major peacetime tasks to perform, a less specialized career cadre would be less eager for wartime. Sweeping though these proposals might be, there is nothing about them that is inherently unfeasible.[6]

Peck argues cogently, "As a people we should not toy with the means of mass destruction without being willing to personally bear the responsibility of wielding them. If we must kill, let us not select and train hired killers to do the dirty job for us and then forget that there's any blood involved."[7]

If such a proposal were implemented and expanded to include a worldwide Peace Corps, the result would be both a more humane military and a less hostile world. The likelihood of war would drop as some of its root causes were attacked. This would be especially true if women were equally represented, and if presidents. congressmen and other policymakers (or their children) were required to serve like everyone else.

Some will complain that a national service corps would simply be a "make-work" program, a black hole for tax dollars. But what is our present military establishment, if not the hugest, most expensive make-work program on earth? In Peck's proposal, the work would be healing and helpful, not destructive and deadening. This is precisely the kind of work we should be creating.

Such changes would not, of course, solve all the dangers of militarization, particularly the nuclear and "Star Wars" technology threats. But they would tend to make the military more humane and accountable, and this is crucial. Peck sets the issue in broad perspective:

> The military-industrial complex that played such a large role in Vietnam, and continues to be a primary creator of the grotesqueness of the arms race, is submitted to nothing but the profit motive. This is no submission at all. It is pure self-interest. I am not an enemy of capitalism per se. I believe it is possible for the profit motive to be operative and at the same time submitted to higher values of truth and love. Difficult, but possible. If we cannot somehow engineer this submission and "Christianize" our capitalism, we are doomed as a capitalist society. The total failure of submission is always evil—for a group, for an institution, for a society as for an individual. Unless we can heal ourselves by submission, the forces of

death will win the day, and we will consume ourselves in our own evil.[8]

This is a kingdom concern, and in this area Christians should be working for kingdom principles. Proposals along this line bear consideration and elaboration by Christians throughout the world.

3. Finding New Models of Economic Life

The church should jump with both feet into the Great Economic Debate raging today[9]—not as defenders of wealth and power, but as advocates for the poor and oppressed. Christians have a unique role to play in shaping future economic policy and arrangements because they can be a strong voice for relieving the oppression of the poor and caring for the environment. One way to help might be through an International Congress on Economics and Social Justice, as Richard Foster has proposed.[10]

J. Andrew Kirk has explored this issue creatively (and biblically) in his book *Good News of the Kingdom Coming*. He notes, "The way that we are conditioned to look at economic matters today is so far from God's will for the human race that it is difficult to know where to begin in the search for genuine changes toward a more equitable society." But he quotes J. H. Oldham's 1926 statement: "When Christians find in the world a state of things which is not in accord with the truth they have learned from Christ, their concern is not that it should be explained but that it should be ended."[11] Kirk notes, quite correctly from the kingdom perspective, that "there cannot be real community where there are great differences of wealth."[12] This is true both in the church and in the community of nations. Christians, therefore, need to work for more equitable alternatives.

To do so, kingdom Christians will need to transcend the capitalist/socialist debate and get back to fundamental kingdom values. Kirk argues,

Again, because Western Christians have often been beneficiaries of the present economic system, they have not been able

to get far enough away from it to see some of the spurious
assumptions on which it is based. The value of the individual,
for example, can in no way be measured by his or her value
in the market. The crisis of escalating unemployment is beginning to bring home to Christian consciences the inadequacies
of a market-economy to meet real human needs, work being
one of the most basic ones.

Free-enterprise economics is often defended on the basis
that it promotes freedom and an open society. This idea, however, is a fallacy. It certainly increases the freedom of some,
but always and inevitably at the expense of the freedom of
others. Freedom is not an ever-expanding commodity. If there
is going to be more real freedom of economic choice (both to
produce and to consume) at the bottom end of society, then
there have to be restrictions placed on the freedoms of those
who can influence economic policies at the top end. . . . Most
of us exist economically on terms laid down by those who
control the international flow of capital. We are far from free
to decide our own priorities and scale of values.[13]

How, then, should Christians respond? Kirk argues, "Whereas
very few, if any, Christians are likely to commit themselves whole-
heartedly to Marxist principles and strategies, they are already
committed, albeit unconsciously at times, to the economic assumptions and values of the capitalist system. If, therefore, they
genuinely want to keep clear of all ideologies, they need con-
sciously to renounce capitalism (in which they are enmeshed)
without accepting Marxism."[14]

Kirk goes on to show some practical ways just economic policies might be derived from a commitment to kingdom priorities.
Much of this is in line with Goudzwaard's suggestions and should
be fed into current Christian contributions to economic debate.

Christians must provide serious analysis to the question of economic systems—analysis grounded in Scripture, not in narrow
North American self-interest. We must see that free-enterprise
capitalism is not just an economic theory; for many it is a theol-

ogy. In place of God is an "invisible hand" (the mystery of the marketplace) which promises to benefit everyone ultimately if each person seeks his or her own self-interest. The irony is that the flat contradiction between this and biblical teaching has not been exposed long since. As Richard Foster observes, "In Christian theology, . . . the only 'invisible hand' is God's, and once we grasp it we discover that it leads away from self-interest to justice and compassion for the poor and oppressed."[15]

Capitalism is a very effective means of concentrating wealth in order to multiply economic dynamism. This is its genius. Yet Christians raise two cautions: First, capitalism relies upon this planet's God-given resources and so is responsible for the stewardship of those resources. Second, wealth accumulation is always a moral danger—as the Gospel reminds us. Concentrating wealth for the sake of economic productivity is necessary and good and can in fact benefit the larger society. But when wealth accumulation operates without restraint and is placed in a sphere of its own morality, it inevitably leads to injustice and the exploitation of the poor.

Fortunately, an increasing number of kingdom-sensitive Christians are raising such issues, and some are beginning to model promising new options. One of the most hopeful is a new business major at Eastern College introduced through the initiative of Anthony Campolo and Ron Sider.

Typically, Christian colleges simply train business majors to find their place and "make it" in the business world, with little concern for ethical issues beyond personal integrity. But the new Eastern College major is something different. Students will be trained to go out and change society through starting new ecologically responsible businesses which will create new jobs for the poor. Studies have shown that most new jobs are created not by large companies but by new, small, high-risk ventures. Campolo hopes to harness the creativity of kingdom-concerned Christians in a kind of sanctified entrepreneurship that will attack some of the root causes of poverty.

This is a good start. Christians should be both seeking and modeling new economic arrangements which are ecologically sensitive, economically viable, labor-intensive and fundamentally just. Much can be done especially in modeling cooperative forms of business ownership which cut the nerve of excessive private wealth accumulation that inevitably leads to the oppression of the have-nots.

4. A Sensible Foreign Policy

Walking the streets of London near Piccadilly Circus, I came upon a cinema showing the American film *Missing*. Seated among the young British crowd, I found it a strange experience as a foreigner to see America's worst side thus exposed to the world's view.

As I watched the film's depiction of U.S. involvement in the overthrow of Salvador Allende in Chile in the early seventies, I asked myself, "Will we ever learn?" Once again the United States had intervened illegally in a Latin American country, and once again the reason was largely economic and political self-interest, very narrowly defined. "Over a period of nearly 150 years, U.S. armed forces [have] swept into Central America and the Caribbean more than 60 times to topple governments, install friendly regimes, aid or suppress revolutions, and support American business interests."[16]

Too often foreign policy is the story of missed opportunities and unjust interventions. Today Central America is a case in point. Besides being a partisan in the protracted civil war in El Salvador, the United States is "covertly" working to overthrow the Sandinista government in Nicaragua. And every American taxpayer helps pay the bill.

Both Nicaragua and Chile reveal the shortsightedness and self-defeating nature of much U.S. foreign policy. In both cases, things could have been different. The Somoza government in Nicaragua was grossly oppressive. A tiny ruling minority controlled both the army and industry, with close ties to U.S. business.

The Sandinista revolution was certainly more a popular revolt than are the current Contra groups. It is not surprising that the Sandinista movement was leftist and was quickly exploited by Marxists. But instead of responding helpfully, with diplomatic recognition, economic aid and favorable trade relations, the U.S. virtually quarantined Nicaragua, much as it did Chile earlier. Not surprisingly, this simply forced the Sandinistas (many Christians among them) closer to the Communist bloc. Meanwhile, the U.S. is arming and funding the Contras, made up, in part, of remnants of Somoza's repressive militia.[17]

If the U.S. had treated Nicaragua fairly and openly, or even as it deals with many non-Communist nations with gross human rights violations (such as the Philippines and Chile), the story could have been different. Today we would be helping Nicaragua in education, health care and other areas, reducing militarization and checking the drift toward totalitarianism. Instead U.S. foreign policy has made Central America an ideological test case between East and West, in the process spending much more on military intervention than would have been necessary for development assistance and loosing a flood of refugees to the U.S. and other countries.

A foreign policy of military intervention is no foreign policy. Generally it is a testimony to the failure of long-range policy based on foresight, understanding, mutual respect, and efforts toward a genuine community of nations.

Kingdom priorities call for foreign policy which respects all peoples and nations and understands that peace, justice and truth worldwide ultimately contribute to one's own self-interest. Christians should work and pray for such policies. The spring for these efforts should be a profound solidarity with our sisters and brothers in Christ in all nations and with the poor and oppressed of the earth. "Do not oppress an alien; you yourselves know how it feels to be aliens, because you were aliens in Egypt" (Ex 23:9).

E. Stanley Jones said years ago that the only sensible principle of relationships among peoples and nations is the principle of cooperation, love in action. Writing of the kingdom, he said:

> Jesus taught that love and love alone was the method. We
> doubt the efficacy of it and turn to force to overcome evil. We
> introduce force into the means hoping we can dismiss it in the
> end. But to our dismay we find that, introduced into the means
> it passes over into the end and corrupts the end. "You cannot
> fight the devil with his fire without yourself getting burned."
> We cannot by some alchemy get the gold of brotherhood out
> of the base metals of hate and force. The only possible way
> to get rid of an enemy is to turn him into a friend—and the
> only possible way to turn him into a friend is to be friendly,
> and to be friendly is to love him.[18]

"Realists" will say that love is fine between individuals but as the
basis for foreign policy it is naive. But a Christian who says this
is saying that ultimately he or she does not really believe in the
present power of the kingdom of God. It is to say Jesus was an
idealist, not a realist. It is to drive an unbiblical wedge between
individual and social morality. As Richard Barnet has written,
"We need to ask why we are doing things collectively that we
would never do individually."[19] Our nations await statesmen and
women with the vision and wisdom to show that love, justice and
cooperation must and can be the foundation of foreign policy.

In this perspective, wise governments will not allow foreign
policy to be dictated by narrow economic or political self-interest.
They will seek to build a genuine community of nations. More,
they will go out of their way to do this, making it a cornerstone
of policy.

In the case of the United States, this might mean identifying
two or three key nations on each continent with which we would
form especially close ties of economic and cultural cooperation.
To some degree, the relationship between the U.S. and Canada
could be the model. The goal would be to create as close ties as
possible with these nations, to work especially to wipe out poverty
there, and to assist these friends to be enablers of help, understanding and cooperation with other nations throughout the re-

gion. These key nations would be chosen not according to racial, ethnic, religious or political criteria, but rather according to their willingness to deal with their own internal needs and to be catalytic good neighbors in the community of nations. In Africa, for example, key nations might be Egypt and Zimbabwe rather than South Africa. On the American continents, certainly close ties and cooperation should be developed with Mexico, Brazil and Argentina.

This international community of nations would seek progressively to provide economic, health and educational assistance, reduce trade barriers, stabilize currencies, eliminate massive debt, introduce and encourage human-scale technology, and work to protect the environment. Some type of multinational developmental Peace Corps might well be formed.

The striking thing about current policy in the Western nations is the absence of such goals and ideals among our political leaders. We see an almost total lack of moral leadership in this sense. Morality has been defined so narrowly, privately and nationalistically that the perspective of God's kingdom is totally eclipsed in the political arena. Today, notes Richard Barnet, "Political leaders secure the approval—or at least the acquiescence—of large majorities of citizens by appealing to the worst within us"; meanwhile U.S. policies "diverge ever more sharply from the best moral traditions of the nation: encouragement of democracy, tolerance of ideological diversity, dedication to international law, and promotion of Third World development. The principles are still professed, but the policies negate the principles." Yet, Barnet warns, "The integrity of a nation, no less than of a man or woman, is measured by how it treats the weak and powerless."[20]

It is time for kingdom-sensitive Christians to articulate and work for sensible, realistic, cooperative foreign policy before it is too late.

5. Rebuilding Urban Neighborhoods

The city is the place of the church's greatest testing today. It is perhaps the world's primary mission field. And kingdom Christians should especially be working there for the justice of God's new order.

A primary task of the church is community building, not only within the church but in the larger human community as well.[21] In its larger dimensions, this means working to rebuild deteriorated urban neighborhoods all around the world.

This is a cooperative task of government, industry, the church and other public-minded groups. Effective strategy begins not with massive government programs (though very substantial public aid is needed) but rather with neighborhood self-help efforts which enable residents to rebuild their own communities.

In the United States, some significant new steps in this direction are being taken by the U.S. Ministry Division of World Vision International. Perhaps this ministry can be an effective catalyst to encourage and energize many of the promising things along this line already being done by hundreds of local churches and other organizations.

The director of World Vision's new U.S. program, J. Paul Landrey, notes that "the program is based upon two interrelated principles: That neighborhood deterioration is essentially an economic condition, so the solution must be to bring economic health to the neighborhood within a holistic setting which also brings spiritual and social healing, and that self-help is the path to that solution."[22] To that end, World Vision has targeted two purposes: (1) to minister to the spiritual, social and physical needs of the poorest and neediest in urban communities, and (2) to enable and empower individual citizens and neighborhood groups to help themselves.

This effort is one among many. Habitat for Humanity is another. Such endeavors hold out hope for a greatly expanded network to rebuild decaying urban communities. The effort will take the cooperation not only of the public and private sectors, but particularly of Christians across the urban-suburban and rich-poor barriers that split the church. This also is kingdom work.

Jerusalem or Babylon?

No one of these efforts, nor all of them combined, constitute *the* project of the kingdom of God. At best, they can point towards God's new order and cooperate with the justice, mercy and truth which God wills. They can help Christians grow beyond ideology into the peace and joy of kingdom life and work.

North American Christians should understand that the United States may be further from the kingdom than they would want to admit. We have thought of the wealth and power of the United States as in some ways signs of God's blessing. But is God pleased with the chasm between the rich and poor nations?

Look at Revelation 18. Babylon is fallen! The mark of Babylon is power and wealth based on international trade. The judgment sounds frightfully modern: "All the nations have drunk the maddening wine of her adulteries. The kings of the earth committed adultery with her, and the merchants of the earth grew rich from her excessive luxuries" (Rev 18:3).

God condemns Babylon and calls his people out of her for "the glory and luxury she gave herself" (Rev 18:7). Time was when her "merchants were the world's great men" (Rev 18:23), when she was the center of international trade in minerals and textiles, grains and manufactured goods, vehicles and luxury items (Rev 18:11-13). But now, judgment.

Certainly North America could never be Babylon. Or could it? Where *is* the city of God? The biblical prophets pronounce the sternest judgment on those people who were blessed by God but failed to keep his covenant. Jerusalem can become Babylon.

The so-called Christian nations may be much closer to the judgment of the kingdom than to its *shalom*. Power and wealth are already there; all that's lacking to fulfill the picture of Revelation 18 is the persecution of the church (Rev 18:24). And it will be surprising, even in "Christian" nations, if those who take up the cross of Christ's kingdom escape persecution.

Because Christians believe that Jesus is life, justice, liberation and truth, and that the church is Jesus' body on earth, they can identify profoundly with Jesus' words: "My Father is always at his work to this very day, and I, too, am working" (Jn 5:17). And yet they can leave the kingdom fully in the Father's hands!

11

The Principles
of the Kingdom

The kingdom of God should shape the church's daily life. Here kingdom vision becomes visible. If this is not so, the church lacks a biblical kingdom vision.

The Scriptures give us kingdom principles for our life together. These are key kingdom realities—basic, practical principles which if ignored or violated *in practice* shortcircuit the kingdom power of the church. They are crucial for genuine, thoroughgoing renewal—the kind of renewal which alone can make the church an instrument of God's kingdom today.

Given the biblical revelation and the contemporary crisis of the church, I would suggest sixteen kingdom operating principles for today.

1. *Unconditional faith in Jesus Christ and obedience to his commands and to the moral law of God as revealed in Scripture.* Jesus said, "If you love me, you will obey what I command" (Jn 14:15). Real faith issues in real obedience. Obedience is deadening if not quickened by a living, vital faith in Jesus Christ. In fact, "this is his command: to believe in the name of his Son, Jesus Christ, and to love one another as he commanded us" (1 Jn 3:23). Don't look

for signs of the kingdom except in a loving community where love flows from faith and obedience.

2. *Consistent, continual communication with God through prayer.* This must mark our life as a Christian community. Only through prayer do we receive our instructions on how, practically, to translate truth into action. Only through prayer do we learn to follow the example of Jesus, who "when he suffered, . . . made no threats" but "entrusted himself to him who judges justly" (1 Pet 2:23). Prayer enables us constantly to keep the kingdom in God's hands.

The need for sustained intercessory prayer on the part of God's people can hardly be overemphasized. Richard Lovelace has recently addressed this, setting forth a "prayer agenda" for global spiritual awakening which includes, among other things, focus on "evangelistic outreach, cultural transformation and the promotion of social justice, . . . calling forth all the gifts of the laity [all God's people] to promote the Kingdom of Christ" so that God's people become "active agents of building Christ's Kingdom, instead of sleepwalking through the world's agendas of success and survival."[1]

Our great kingdom prayer priorities, in fact, are threefold. I was impressed with this recently in my own prayer time. These priorities are (1) the world renewal and unity of the body of Christ, that we all may be one, that the world may know the truth of Jesus (Jn 17:23); (2) world evangelism, that all peoples may hear and understand the gospel, and faithful disciples be made in all nations (Mt 28:19-20); and (3) world justice, that the poor and oppressed may be relieved and given life, and that the promise that Messiah shall establish "justice on earth" (Is 42:4) may be fulfilled. These should be the focus of our prayers to God.

3. *Biblically defined leadership* as pictured in 1 Timothy 3:1-13, Titus 1:5-9 and similar passages. Too often we choose leaders for the wrong reasons, or we choose the wrong leaders because we fail to apply the qualifications clearly given us in Scripture. This shortcircuits renewal.

How many times I have seen a church choose leaders without even passing reference to biblical qualifications! This undercuts the renewing work of the Spirit much more than we realize, because leaders who are insensitive to kingdom priorities often fail to operate on kingdom principles. The question is never simply, Who will do the job? It is always, Whom is God choosing for this task? Leadership should be given to women and men "who are known to be full of the Spirit and wisdom" (Acts 6:3).

4. *Plural or shared pastoral leadership in each congregation.* The consistent New Testament pattern is a shared leadership among all those whom God gifts and raises up as leaders—not the one-man pastoral expert. Nowhere is the idea of one pastor over a congregation upheld in Scripture.

In the New Testament the apostles initially appointed "elders" (plural) "in each church" (Acts 14:23); later congregations apparently chose their own elders. The task of these leaders was pastoral: to "direct the affairs of the church," including the work of "preaching and teaching" (1 Tim 5:17). The head of the church is Jesus, never a human pastor. And Jesus rules in each congregation not through one person but through a pastoral team which operates as New Testament elders did.

Contemporary churches need not have elders in precisely the New Testament sense, or use the term, but any church which fails to have the functional equivalent of eldership and make plural leadership the norm is to that degree not a biblical church. Its leadership will thus be less effective from the kingdom perspective.

Plural leadership is neither mere pragmatics nor remote New Testament practice. A deeper principle is involved. God wants leaders (1) who are mature and sensitive to his Spirit and (2) who discern God's will *together* in shared leadership. This pattern serves as a safeguard against the limited wisdom and perception (as well as the fragile or too robust ego) of one leader only.

5. *Decision making by Spirit-guided consensus in the church and in the home,* rather than by either authoritarian dictate or by simple

majority vote. Frequently when the majority rules, the Spirit doesn't. It is Jesus' task to lead the church; it is the church's task to discern God's will and obey. God reveals his will through consensus among the pastoral leadership and, on major issues, through consensus in the whole body. The task of leaders is to help the church understand and follow what God is saying. This includes helping the larger church come to consensus on God's will regarding specific issues. There is little danger of a church going wrong where leaders and people, open to the Spirit and grounded in the Word, are agreed on the proper course of action. However, linkage of congregations in larger networks provides added strengths and safeguards.

Since the church is the family of God and the family is the church of God, the same principles hold in the home as in the church. Jesus is the head, and the parents (the "elders" in the family, in most cases) are to lead the home through mutually discerning and applying God's will. Thus what happens in home and church are not two different things. Each household is a minichurch, and the same general principles apply.

6. *The Christian ministry as a stewardship committed to all believers,* male and female, rich and poor, educated and uneducated. In God's kingdom, every believer serves as a minister and priest of the gospel (1 Cor 12:4-7; 1 Pet 2:4-9). The New Testament does not divide up people as "ministers" and "laymen," but pictures the church as a serving community with "different kinds of service" (1 Cor 12:5).

All believers are ministers of the kingdom, agents of the new order. The church will never be the church and the kingdom will never come in power until believers accept the stewardship of the call and gifts God has given (see 1 Pet 4:10).

7. *Equipping believers for ministry based on their gifts, common priesthood and spiritual growth, as the principal task of church leadership.* The number one priority of pastoral leadership is to prepare God's people for ministry (Eph 4:12), whether by preaching, discipling, prayer, coordinating or other means.

Believers have already been called and baptized into the ministry, but they need to be trained and equipped. Thus the defining task of leadership is equipping for ministry.[2] Effective sergeants don't train their troops to watch the fight, and good coaches aren't mainly interested in providing cheerleaders. Pastors who don't produce ministers betray the kingdom.

8. *A preferential concern for the poor in the church's life, ministry and theology.* As B. T. Roberts insisted, ministry to and among the poor is the "crowning proof" of faithful witness: "In this respect the Church must follow in the footsteps of Jesus."[3]

We saw earlier Jesus' own identification with the Jubilee theme and the biblical theme of justice for the poor. So this concern goes to the heart of the nature of the kingdom. The church's visible concern for the poor is both an indicator of faithfulness and a sign of the kingdom.

A biblical concern for the poor will always keep the requirements of justice before the church, for it is the church's task to side with the victims of injustice and to maintain their rights, even while calling them to repentance, faith and discipleship.

9. *Grounding the church's life and theology in real Christian community with a balance among worship, community and witness.* Biblically the church is by definition a community, not an institution. In fact, it is a *countercultural* community, the embryonic community of the kingdom, distinct from surrounding society at every point where that society is in bondage to the "basic principles of this world" (Col 2:8, 20).[4]

The church's task is to build such community according to kingdom principles. This can be done; in many cases it simply is not being done because of ignorance and lack of visible models of kingdom communities. But in many places, this is changing.[5]

In *Liberating the Church* I have developed at some length a model of church life based on the three primary functions of worship, community (koinonia) and witness. These are the areas to which the church should be especially directing its attention in these days. Worship: the "missing jewel" in many evangelical churches.[6] Community: the building of biblical Christian counterculture.[7] Witness: the church's prophetic life in the world, where Jesus-style *doing* is grounded in *being* the body of Christ.

10. *Small-group structures through which commitments and beliefs are translated into action.* This is the only hope for closing the discipleship gap in the church. The church will be a kingdom community only as it develops *committed personal relationships* within the body. Clearly, in today's world this requires some form of cell or small group. To be faithful to the kingdom, the church *must* find the context where believers can "encourage one another daily" (Heb 3:13) and "spur one another on toward love and good deeds" (Heb 10:24). Hebrews 10:25 makes clear that such intimate community requires "meeting together" with frequency and intimacy. Once-a-week large-group worship is not enough to prevent the subversion of the church.

11. *Mutual submission as the fundamental principle of all relationships in the home and the church.* Mutual submission is a key to servanthood and essential to real Christian love. The many "one another" passages in the New Testament show that the health of the Christian community depends on mutual submission. We are to "accept one another" (Rom 15:7), "serve one another" (Gal 5:13), "bear with" and "forgive" one another (Col 3:13), clothe ourselves with humility toward one another (1 Pet 5:5), and in all things "submit to one another out of reverence for Christ" (Eph 5:21). This is, of course, precisely what Jesus taught and modeled for us. This principle must operate in all Christian relationships, whether in the church, the home or the marketplace.

12. *Openness to the exercise of all the biblical gifts of the Spirit, without restriction on the basis of sex, status, age, education or leadership role.* The New Testament puts much less restriction on the free course of spiritual gifts than do most churches today. Yet one cannot have a church which is paralyzed in gifts and yet potent for the kingdom. Churches must encourage, affirm and facilitate as many spiritual gifts as the Spirit bestows.

An effective church will welcome and encourage—and also discipline and guide—the gifts of women and men, young and old, rich and poor, new convert and seasoned saint. It will bring forth gifts in all the areas of church life, whether worship, community or witness. This very diversity is, in fact, a visible sign of the kingdom. The kingdom age is the age of Pentecost, when the Holy Spirit has been poured out on all believers (Acts 2:17).

13. *A commitment to evangelism and the discipling of new converts* as the first priority of the church's witness in the world.[8] A proper biblical kingdom emphasis heightens rather than lessens the priority of evangelism, for kingdom Christians strive to win the allegiance of people *now* to Jesus Christ, both for kingdom work now and for their eternal salvation. Evangelism does not always come *before* other forms of witness, but it is ultimately more important and must never be slighted. On the other hand, evangelism is not exclusively the call to initial conversion, but the proclamation of the kingdom in all its fullness. Thus justice ministries are one form of proclaiming the kingdom, and evangelism is one form of social action.

Since the goal of evangelism is disciples, not converts (Mt 28:19-20), the church must lead new believers on to spiritual maturity and significant kingdom ministry consistent with their gifts. Thus evangelism links with equipping all believers for ministry.

14. *The exercise of discipline and mutual admonition within the church according to New Testament principles.* This is closely related to several of the above points, particularly numbers 10 and 11. Jesus gives clear principles for exercising discipline in the church (Mt 18:15-18), and to neglect these is simply to ratify the church's accommodation to the world. An undisciplined church eventually ends up not being a kingdom community at all, but only a bastion of civil religion. A key role of leadership is to see that discipline operates according to the principles of the kingdom.[9]

How can we exercise discipline effectively, without legalism, in an undisciplined, individualistic age? John R. Martin has given some thought to this and wisely comments:

I believe an effective model would be admonition based on accountability. This model assumes that: (1) biblical discipleship is a dynamic following of the risen Christ, not following a predefined order; (2) members of congregations are at various levels of spiritual maturity; and (3) most members live below the level of their spiritual understanding. The model I am proposing would see the primary function of admonition as helping another Christian to clarify his or her spiritual understanding and to become accountable to live that level of knowledge through the grace and power of God. The primary task of the person doing the admonishing is to help the other person live the truth God has shown him or her, not to dictate the details of their life or to enforce a defined order.[10]

15. *Maintaining a clear corporate witness against the idolatries of the present age.* The Bible is persistent in its denunciation of idolatry. Yet Christians today, especially in the nations of power and affluence, are idolators more often than they know. The New Testament warns that idolators will not inherit the kingdom of God and that greed is a principal form of idolatry (Gal 5:20; Eph 5:5; Col 3:5).

The idols of our time, as Bob Goudzwaard has prophetically shown, are especially the ideologies of revolution, nation, material prosperity and guaranteed security. For these, many Christians today are ready to sacrifice the weightier matters of the kingdom: justice, mercy and truth. In North America, for instance, fundamental kingdom values of justice and health for the world's poor are being systematically sacrificed on the altars of supposed national security or "superiority" by literally millions of Bible-quoting Christians.

Many Christians, says Goudzwaard, "have selected their own goals, delivered themselves over to various ideologies, and thus have unwittingly worshiped demonic powers. They have built their own empire rather than God's kingdom." Thus a "great tension exists . . . between following Jesus and serving idols," and we face the choice either to relativize our ideological goals or to relativize biblical norms.[11]

God's kingdom concerns sovereignty, allegiance and first priorities here on earth now. Standing in clear opposition to the idolatrous ideologies of our time therefore is a key to building kingdom communities.

16. *A commitment to the body of Christ, the church throughout the world, which surpasses our allegiance to our own nation, political or economic system, or ideology.* When we identify more with suffering Christians in Africa or El Salvador than with American forces in scattered Third World nations, for example, we will know we are beginning to catch a kingdom vision.

Today too many Christians put their national, racial or economic identity above their identity as citizens of jesus' new order. This is simply wrong. it always leads to supporting nationalistic or economic priorities over kingdom priorities. We must come to an awareness of God's kingdom community as one people, one nation, one new race throughout the world, with one primary allegiance to Christ our King. National, military and economic conflicts look much different from this side of the fence.

These principles are simply ways of applying the basic themes of the kingdom to the daily life of the church. The church must *now* begin to model, by the grace of God, the peaceable kingdom of justice and righteousness in the earth. It must *now* show itself to be the embryo of the house and city of God where Sabbath and Jubilee begin. This is the way to God's kingdom *now*.

I am convinced these principles point in the right direction for kingdom faithfulness in the church. Many of them are grossly violated in the majority of North American churches. Applying them would have a revolutionary impact across the board in the church. They would liberate the church from its preoccupation with church business, freeing it for kingdom business.

Conclusion
Traditionally the kingdom of God has been treated as a question

of eschatology. It has been introduced last as something to consider after all other doctrines have been treated. But where did we get the idea that our theology should *end* with the kingdom, when Jesus *began* with it?

Under the influence of current world conditions, the emergence of the "theology of hope" and other currents, eschatology has in recent decades moved from the end to the beginning of the theological agenda. This is proper, for the kingdom of God provides the overarching biblical framework for our lives and our faith as Christians. The fundamental reality is God; the most basic question is how we live our lives before him. And the kingdom of God, centering in the life, death, resurrection and reign of Jesus Christ, provides the answer.

The recovery of kingdom hope is crucial for the church in general and for evangelical theology in particular. If we can be fully biblical in pursuing this theme, we can see an unprecedented inbreaking of God's kingdom in the present age and a hastening of the day when the kingdoms of this world will become the kingdom of our Lord and of his Christ.

And so I close with a prayer, in the words of Charles Wesley:

Father of everlasting love,
   To every soul thy Son reveal,
Our guilt and sufferings to remove,
   Our deep, original wound to heal;
And bid the fallen race arise,
   And turn our earth to Paradise.

Let the church be the children of the kingdom: Those who pray, "Your will be done on earth." And then do it.

Select Bibliography

Adeney, Miriam. *God's Foreign Policy*. Grand Rapids, Michigan: Eerdmans, 1984.

Arias, Mortimer. *Announcing the Reign of God: Evangelization and the Subversive Memory of Jesus*. Philadelphia: Fortress Press, 1984.

Berry, Wendell. *The Unsettling of America: Culture and Agriculture*. New York: Avon Books, 1978.

Costas, Orlando E. *Christ Outside the Gate: Mission Beyond Christendom*. Maryknoll, New York: Orbis, 1982.

Foster, Richard J. *Freedom of Simplicity*. New York: Harper and Row, 1981.

Goudzwaard, Bob. *Idols of Our Time*. Downers Grove, Illinois: InterVarsity, 1984.

Guelich, Robert A. *The Sermon on the Mount*. Waco, Texas: Word, 1982.

Hanks, Thomas. *God So Loved the Third World: The Biblical Vocabulary of Oppression*. Maryknoll, New York: Orbis, 1983.

Jones, E. Stanley. *Is the Kingdom of God Realism?* New York: Abingdon-Cokesbury, 1940.

Kirk, J. Andrew. *Good News of the Kingdom Coming*. Downers Grove, Illinois: InterVarsity, 1985.

Kraybill, Donald B. *The Upside-Down Kingdom*. Scottdale, Pennsylvania: Herald Press, 1978.

Martin, John R. *Ventures in Discipleship: A Handbook for Groups or Individuals*. Scottdale, Pennsylvania: Herald Press, 1984.

Newbigin, Lesslie. *Sign of the Kingdom*. Grand Rapids, Michigan: Eerdmans, 1980.

Peck, M. Scott. *People of the Lie: The Hope for Healing Human Evil*. New York: Simon and Schuster, 1983.

Ronsvale, John and Sylvia. *The Hidden Billions: The Potential of the Church in the U.S.A.* Champaign, Illinois: C-4 Resources, 1984.

Sloan, Robert B., Jr. *The Favorable Year of the Lord*. Austin, Texas: Schola Press, 1977.

Yoder, John Howard. *The Politics of Jesus*. Grand Rapids, Michigan: Eerdmans, 1972.

Notes

Preface

[1]Interview with Richard C. Halverson, *Decision* 26:1 (January 1985), p. 24.

[2]George Barna with William P. McKay, *Vital Signs: Emerging Social Trends and the Future of American Christianity*(Westchester, IL: Crossway Books, 1984), p.5.

Introduction: A Key to All of Scripture

[1]A selection of some of the more significant recent writings on the kingdom and related themes is included in the bibliography at the end of this book.

[2]Richard F. Lovelace, "Thy Kingdom Come on Earth and in Heaven" (1982 Colloquy on the Hallowing of Life, Notre Dame, Indiana), p. 2.

[3]John Bright, *The Kingdom of God* (Nashville: Abingdon, 1953), p. 7.

[4]E. Stanley Jones, *Is the Kingdom of God Realism?* (New York: Abingdon-Cokesbury, 1940), p. 53. As Mortimer Arias has noted, Jones was "a notable exception" to the tendency to neglect the kingdom theme and "gladly acknowledged he was 'obsessed' with the kingdom of God, and . . . consistently tried for half a century to present the gospel in that perspective" (Mortimer Arias, *Announcing the Reign of God: Evangelization and the Subversive Memory of Jesus* [Philadelphia: Fortress Press, 1984], p. 123).

[5]Note, for example, 1 Corinthians 4:20, 15:24-28; Colossians 1:13; Romans 14:17, 15:12 and other references. While Romans 8:20-22 does not explicitly use kingdom language, it is clearly kingdom material.

1 The Peaceable Order

[1]As *shalom* or its derivatives, not counting proper names. See Douglas J. Harris, *Shalom! The Biblical Concept of Peace* (Grand Rapids: Baker, 1970), pp. 13-24.

[2]Ibid., p. 14.

[3]John V. Taylor, *Enough Is Enough* (Minneapolis: Augsburg Publishing

House, 1977), p. 42.

⁴See Gerhard von Rad, *Old Testament Theology,* trans. D. M. G. Stalker, 2 vols. (New York: Harper and Row, 1962), 1:130.

⁵Von Rad in Gerhard Kittel, ed., *Theological Dictionary of the New Testament,* trans. Geoffrey W. Bromiley, 10 vols. (Grand Rapids: Eerdmans, 1964-76), 2:402-3 (hereafter cited as Kittel, *TDNT*).

⁶Ibid., pp. 414, 412.

⁷John Wesley, *Explanatory Notes upon the New Testament* (London: Epworth Press, 1958), p. 29.

⁸Walter Brueggemann, *Living Toward a Vision: Biblical Reflections of Shalom* (Philadelphia: United Church Press, 1976), p. 16.

⁹Ibid., p. 19.

2 The Promised Land

¹Wendell Berry, *The Unsettling of America* (New York: Avon Books, 1978), pp. 7-8.

²Walter Brueggemann, *The Land* (Philadelphia: Fortress Press, 1977), pp. 2-3, Brueggemann's emphasis. This is, however, a little overstated.

³Ibid.

⁴To inherit the land or earth is a common biblical theme, as a study of the word *inherit* will show.

⁵Colin Brown, ed., *The New International Dictionary of New Testament Theology,* 3 vols. (Grand Rapids: Zondervan, 1975), 1:517.

⁶Ibid., p. 518.

⁷The Greek of Matthew 5:5 is virtually word-for-word identical with the Greek (Septuagint) version of Psalm 37:11 (note also Ps 37:9). In both cases the word for earth/land is *gē*.

⁸It is relevant here to note the significant "theology of restoration" or restitution in Peter's sermons and letters. Note especially Acts 2:17; 3:19-21; 1 Peter 5:10; 2 Peter 3:13. This is consistent with Paul's theology, as, for example, in Romans 8, and underscores the kingdom theme.

3 The House of God

¹Howard A. Snyder, *The Problem of Wineskins: Church Structure in a Technological Age* (Downers Grove, Ill.: InterVarsity, 1975).

²See the fuller discussion in *The Problem of Wineskins,* pp. 57-65.

³See *Liberating the Church: The Ecology of Church and Kingdom* (Downers Grove, Ill.: InterVarsity, 1983), chapters two and three.

4 The City of the King

¹Jacques Ellul, *The Meaning of the City* (Grand Rapids: Eerdmans, 1970). See

also Harvie Conn's essays in Roger Greenway, ed., *Discipling the City: Theological Reflections on Urban Mission* (Grand Rapids: Baker, 1979).

²Ellul, *The Meaning of the City*, p. 5.

5 Justice for the Poor

¹As I have argued in *The Problem of Wineskins*, pp. 37-53, and in *Liberating the Church*, pp. 235-45.

²Especially helpful here is Thomas Hanks, *God So Loved the Third World* (Maryknoll, N.Y.: Orbis, 1983).

³John Wesley, Sermon, "Justification by Faith," *The Works of John Wesley*, ed. Frank Baker, vol. 1 (Nashville: Abingdon Press, 1984), p. 189.

⁴*Liberating the Church*, pp. 25-26; compare with Kittel, *TDNT*, 3:927.

⁵See the discussion in *TDNT*, 3:923-33.

⁶Ibid., p. 931.

⁷This does not mean that justice is necessarily synonymous with equality, for justice is an ethical and moral *quality* of rightness, while equality implies *quantitative* relationship. Certainly justice demands racial "equality," for example, yet in some contexts preferential treatment (not just technical equality) may be the requirement of justice. Again, justice does not necessarily require strict equality in wealth or standard of living, but it does require that all people have their basic needs for food, shelter, self-respect and purposeful activity met.

6 The Age of Sabbath

¹Kittel, *TDNT*, 7:8. Abraham Heschel notes that the Ten Commandments establish a sacred time, but not a sacred place. See note 2, below.

²Abraham J. Heschel, *Between God and Man: An Interpretation of Judaism*, edited by Fritz A. Rothschild (New York: The Free Press, 1959, 1965), p. 216.

³This is not to drive a wedge between history and nature; God wills through history, through his people, to show the goodness of the created order and bring its full liberation (Rom 8:21), and the material world, as we shall see, is the environment where God's *shalom* is revealed.

⁴Heschel, *Between God and Man*, p. 216.

⁵This does not mean eternity is merely endless time; the environment of the kingdom finally established will be a new order of reality which our concepts of neither time nor eternity are fully able to comprehend.

7 The Age of Jubilee

¹Hanks, *God So Loved the Third World*, pp. 97-104. Note also the Jubilee character of Psalm 146:7-9.

²See Robert North, *Sociology of the Biblical Jubilee* (Rome, 1954); Sharon Ringe,

"The Jubilee Proclamation in the Ministry and Teaching of Jesus" (Ph.D. diss., Union, 1981); Robert Sloan, "The Favorable Year of the Lord" (D. Theol. diss., Basel, 1977).

[3]So argues André Trocmé in *Jesus and the Nonviolent Revolution*, trans. Michael Shank and Marlin Miller (Scottdale, Penn.: Herald Press, 1973), pp. 39-40.

[4]Mortimer Arias, "The Jubilee: A Paradigm for Mission Today," typescript copy, p. 4. See also Arias, *Announcing the Reign of God*.

[5]John Howard Yoder, *The Politics of Jesus* (Grand Rapids: Eerdmans, 1972), pp. 64-77.

[6]Lesslie Newbigin, *Sign of the Kingdom* (Grand Rapids: Eerdmans, 1980), p. 29.

[7]Ibid., p. 30.

[8]See, for example, Ringe, "The Jubilee Proclamation," pp. 243-58.

[9]Robert A. Guelich, *The Sermon on the Mount* (Waco, Tex.: Word, 1982), pp. 70-76.

[10]See Sloan, "The Favorable Year of the Lord," pp. 15-16, 55.

[11]Arias, "The Jubilee," p. 16.

[12]John M. Perkins, "Leadership for Justice in the Black Community," *Urban Mission* 1:1 (September 1983), pp. 12-13.

[13]Newbigin, *Sign of the Kingdom*, p. 38.

[14]Millennial theories may be seen as attempts to solve and dissolve this mystery of the kingdom by resolving all paradoxes into a consistent, rational system. But more is lost than gained in this attempt. Finally, the mystery of the kingdom will not be resolved by our theories but only in our experience of the kingdom—partially now, and fully when the kingdom comes in completion.

8 The People of the Kingdom

[1]Marilee Pierce Dunker, *Man of Vision, Woman of Prayer* (Nashville: Thomas Nelson, 1980).

[2]Quoted in Richard J. Foster, *Freedom of Simplicity* (New York: Harper and Row, 1981), p. 55. (Language slightly modernized.)

[3]Jones, *Is the Kingdom of God Realism?* pp. 58-59.

[4]Protestant theology has tended to understand "body of Christ" quite abstractly and metaphorically, rather than affirming the realism and visible social reality of this idea as it appears in the New Testament.

[5]Harold S. Bender, "Walking in the Resurrection," *The Mennonite Quarterly Review* 35 (April 1961), pp. 108-9.

[6]This is vividly reinforced throughout the New Testament, most pointedly in Romans 12 and 1 Corinthians 12.

[7]See particularly *The Community of the King* and *Liberating the Church*, which

include references to a number of significant works on the church

[8]Some object to closely linking evangelism and justice concerns lest we add a new legalism to the gospel (that is, that social action is necessary for salvation) or imply that good works (social action, in this case) are necessary for salvation. The answer here is to focus not on human obligation first of all, but on God's action. God has graciously intervened in history to bring redemption and liberation through Jesus Christ. Our response is to be both worship and witness, and witness includes both evangelism and justice ministry. An emphasis on social ministry is no more an emphasis on works than is an emphasis on evangelism. Both are, first of all, God's action and, secondarily, our human response, out of love and obedience, to God's action. The two are, in fact, in kingdom perspective, all part of the same picture. The gospel is the good news of God's redemption and restoration of humankind and the whole created order, and this involves both evangelism and justice. Conversely, neither evangelism nor justice is a work which merits our salvation, which is by grace alone. All redemption comes by God's grace, whether that of individual persons, society or the environment.

9 The Possibility of the Kingdom

[1]Note the many prophecies in Isaiah and Revelation, for instance, concerning the wealth, luxury and commerce of nations, as well as Jesus' frequent teachings on economic matters.

[2]Thus I am not presupposing anthropological monism, but merely affirming the biblical mystery of human personhood, which ultimately defies our analysis and dissection.

[3]Jones, *Is the Kingdom of God Realism?* pp. 59-60. In this book I stress, as did Jones, *both* the gradual and the cataclysmic coming of the kingdom, though without commitment to any particular millennial or dispensational theory. For biblical, historical and logical reasons, I have problems with both premillennial and postmillennial theories, which are extrabiblical and have often done as much harm as good in the church by making void parts of the Word of God by an interpretive tradition.

The kingdom, as I understand Scripture, comes *both* as process and as climax, and it is all of grace, through Jesus Christ. My view is not the naive optimism of late nineteenth and early twentieth-century kingdom theologies, for it takes sin seriously in both its personal and structural dimensions, insists on the importance of conversion, and depends finally on the return of Christ. Its optimism rests in the power of God's victory through Jesus Christ.

[4]John Wesley, "The General Spread of the Gospel," *The Works of John Wesley,* ed. Thomas Jackson, 3d ed., 1872, vol. 6 (Peabody, Mass.: Hendrickson

Publishers reprint, 1984), pp. 282-83.

[5]Ibid., p. 283.

[6]Richard N. Ostling, "A Church in Crisis Weeps and Prays," _Time_ 124:12 (September 17, 1984), p. 74.

10 The Project of the Kingdom

[1]Bob Goudzwaard, _Idols of Our Time_ (Downers Grove, Ill.: InterVarsity, 1984), pp. 106-7. This policy is not inconsistent with maintaining a strong military defense (as distinct from actively preparing for massive civilian devastation).

[2]Ibid., p. 107.

[3]Pat Robertson, _The Secret Kingdom_ (Nashville: Thomas Nelson, 1982), p. 133.

[4]M. Scott Peck, _People of the Lie: The Hope for Healing Human Evil_ (New York: Simon and Schuster, 1983), pp. 231-32.

[5]Ibid., p. 232.

[6]Ibid., p. 238.

[7]Ibid., p. 232.

[8]Ibid., p. 252.

[9]See J. Philip Wogaman, _The Great Economic Debate: An Ethical Analysis_ (Philadelphia: Westminster Press, 1977), and my _Liberating the Church_, pp. 52-67.

[10]Foster, _Freedom of Simplicity_, p. 178.

[11]J. Andrew Kirk, _Good News of the Kingdom Coming_ (Downers Grove, Ill.: InterVarsity, 1985), p. 76.

[12]Ibid., p. 77.

[13]Ibid.

[14]Ibid., p. 79.

[15]Foster, _Freedom of Simplicity_, p. 174. See also Bob Goudzwaard, _Capitalism and Progress_ (Grand Rapids: Eerdmans, 1979), especially pp. 27-29.

[16]Susanna McBee, _U.S. News and World Report_, October 17, 1983, quoted in Charles Clements, M.D., _Witness to War: An American Doctor in El Salvador_ (New York: Bantam, 1984), p. 278. Clements's book shows the parallels between U.S. involvement in Vietnam and in Central America. He holds that official government information concerning Central America today is no more reliable than the information provided during the Vietnam era.

[17]Some forty-five of the top fifty officers of the Contra forces are reportedly former officers of Somoza's notorious national guard.

[18]Jones, _Is the Kingdom of God Realism?_ pp. 171-72.

[19]Richard J. Barnet, "Losing Moral Ground: The Foundations of U.S. Foreign Policy," _Sojourners_ 14:3 (March 1985), p. 27.

[20]Ibid., pp. 24, 28.

[21]See _Liberating the Church_, pp. 127-31.

[22]J. Paul Landrey, "Giving Life to Dreams," _Bridges_ 1:1 (Summer 1984), p. 1.

11 The Principles of the Kingdom

[1]Richard Lovelace, "Renewal, Prayer and World Evangelization," *Renewal* 4:1 (August 1984), p. 14.

[2]See *Liberating the Church,* chapter 15.

[3]B. T. Roberts, "Free Churches," *The Earnest Christian* 1:1 (January 1860), p. 7.

[4]See my discussion of the church as countercultural community in chapter five of *Liberating the Church.*

[5]Much useful practical pastoral wisdom for building kingdom communities is coming from communities which are struggling with this task. See such publications as *Sojourners* and *Coming Together,* 414 W. Wolf St., Elkhart, IN 46515.

[6]See "The Church's Missing Jewel" and other chapters on worship in George Mallone, *Furnace of Renewal: A Vision for the Church* (Downers Grove, Ill.: InterVarsity, 1981).

[7]See John R. W. Stott, *The Message of the Sermon on the Mount: Christian Counter-Culture* (Downers Grove, Ill.: InterVarsity, 1978).

[8]See *Liberating the Church,* pp. 149-50.

[9]For an excellent recent discussion of this subject, see John White and Ken Blue, *Healing the Wounded: The Costly Love of Church Discipline* (Downers Grove, Ill.: InterVarsity, 1985).

[10]John R. Martin, *Ventures in Discipleship: A Handbook for Groups or Individuals* (Scottdale, Penn.: Herald Press, 1984), p. 67.

[11]Goudzwaard, *Idols of Our Time,* pp. 76-77.

Scripture Index